VARIATIONS
COOKBOOK
MEAT & POULTRY

Abbreviations and Quantities

1 oz	= 1 ounce = 28 grams
1 lb	= 1 pound = 16 ounces
1 cup	= approx. 5-8 ounces *(depending on density)
1 cup	= 8 fluid ounces = 250 milliliters (liquids)
2 cups	= 1 pint (liquids)
8 pints	= 4 quarts = 1 gallon (liquids)
1 g	= 1 gram = $^1/_{1000}$ kilogram
1 kg	= 1 kilogram = 1000 grams = $2^1/_4$ lb
1 l	= 1 liter = 1000 milliliters (ml) = approx. 34 fluid ounces
125 milliliters (ml)	= approx. 8 tablespoons = $^1/_2$ cup
1 tbsp	= 1 level tablespoon = 15-20 g *(depending on density)
	= 15 milliliters (liquids)
1 tsp	= 1 level teaspoon = 3-5 g *(depending on density) = 5 ml (liquids)

*The weight of dry ingredients varies significantly depending on the density factor, e.g. 1 cup flour weighs less than 1 cup butter. Quantities in ingredients have been rounded up or down for convenience, where appropriate. Metric conversions may not therefore correspond exactly. It is important to use either American or metric measurements within a recipe.

British Cookery Terms

US	UK	US	UK
arugula	rocket salad	molasses	treacle
bacon slices	streaky bacon, streaky rashers	offal	variety meats
beet	beetroot	papaya	pawpaw
bouillon cube	stock cube	parsley root	Hamburg parsley
broil, broiler	grill, oven grill	peanut, peanut oil	groundnut, groundnut oil
chicory	endive	pit	stone (of fruits)
cilantro	fresh coriander leaves	porcini mushrooms	ceps, boletus or penny bun
coconut, shredded or grated	desiccated coconut	powdered sugar	icing sugar
cookie	biscuit (sweet)	rise	prove
corn	maize, sweetcorn	rutabaga	Swede
cornstarch	cornflour	seed	pip
eggplant	aubergine	shrimp	prawn
flour, all-purpose	plain flour	silvered almonds	flaked almonds
French fries	chips	snow peas, sugar peas	mangetout
golden raisins	sultanas	Swiss chard	chard
grill	barbecue	tart	flan
ground beef or pork	minced meat or mince	tofu	beancurd
ham (cured)	gammon	tomato paste	tomato puree
heavy (whipping) cream	double cream	whole wheat	wholemeal
jelly	jam	zucchini	courgette

© h.f.ullmann publishing GmbH
Original title: *Variationenkochbuch. Fleisch & Geflügel*
ISBN of the original edition: 978-3-8331-5864-3

Design, photography, layout, and typesetting: TLC Digitales Fotostudio GmbH & Co KG, Velen-Ramsdorf
Editors: Bettina Snowdon, Sylvia Winnewisser
Copy editing: Annerose Sieck
© for this English edition:
h.f.ullmann publishing GmbH

Translation from German: Susan James in association with First Edition Translations Ltd, Cambridge, UK
Editing: Sally Heavens in association with First Edition Translations Ltd, Cambridge, UK
Typesetting: Rob Partington in association with First Edition Translations Ltd, Cambridge, UK
Cover design: Hubert Hepfinger
Overall responsibility for production: h.f.ullmann publishing GmbH, Potsdam, Germany

ISBN 978-3-8480-0011-1

Printed in China

10 9 8 7 6 5 4 3 2 1
X IX VIII VII VI V IV III II I

www.ullmann-publishing.com
newsletter@ullmann-publishing.com

VARIATIONS
COOKBOOK
MEAT & POULTRY

More than 200 basic recipes and variations

h.f.ullmann

CONTENTS

INTRODUCTION

This book contains an innovative collection of recipes, intended to give imaginative cooks plenty of scope for trying out new ideas.

As well as recipes for classic dishes, you will find numerous unusual variations.

Take your time to browse through the following pages, read the recommendations and advice in the introduction, and then go find your favorite meat recipe.

The text contains information on all you need for cooking, and how to do it. The photographs are meant to make your mouth water.

And now we'll wish you every success—and bon appétit!

ABOUT THIS BOOK

Why this book?

We've all been there. Veal is on special offer, the butcher has tender lamb chops, and the organic shop has an offer on the fresh free-range chicken.

You're standing in the fresh meats aisle of the supermarket and thinking of a delicious Sunday roast, a juicy cutlet, or perhaps crispy grilled meat skewers for your next barbecue, and your mouth is already watering. It's so hard to decide. But when, at last, you've finished your shopping and arrived home, what next? You wonder how you can best prepare the tasty-looking meat you've just bought. Braise it, stew it, roast it, or broil it... which is best?

How long do you need to fry a steak, so that it ends up medium while remaining nice and juicy? And which sauces go well with pork medallions?

Our own repertoire of recipes is often limited—particularly if we want to put something different on the table and not the meals we usually serve. A good cookbook now would be worth its weight in gold! Most cookbooks offer a maximum of one or two ways of preparing a particular dish, and they might just about manage one version of a side dish, salad, or sauce—not enough to try out something new.

Advantages

This cookbook is different. It starts at the very point where other cookbooks stop—with variations on the recipes.

This means you won't find just one recipe for chops, for example, but at least four variations providing different options. You'll find a wide selection of side dishes such as potato, pasta, rice, and vegetable recipes, which you can try out just as you please. For sauce and gravy fans, we also recommend both classic sauces and unusual, not exactly everyday, sauces or dips for almost every dish.

You can also find useful advice and information on the individual ingredients.

Viewed in this way, the book becomes something like a set of building blocks for innovative cooks.

How to use this book

This is how it's put together: this book of meat cookery is divided into four chapters, with titles that reflect the various cooking methods, such as quick-frying or braising, but also particular kinds of meat, such as poultry and ground meat.

For each type of dish, there is a basic—generally, a classic—recipe, which you might always have wanted to get to know in details. For this recipe, the step by step cooking instructions and photographs give you that opportunity. Also on this page, you can find either information on one of the ingredients, or recipes for the side dish.

The double page spread that follows shows between four and six options for varying the basic recipe, also with a good, clear photograph for each one. As a little extra, we also introduce you either to more side dishes, such as potatoes, rice, pasta, polenta, vegetables, or salads—or to delicious sauces that you can do individually, but also vary according to your own ideas. We have collected the recipes to cover a wide range of tastes from all cuisines, all over the world.

You are now well equipped to surprise your family, friends and neighbours with a meal that they won't have eaten every day.

We wish you plenty of success in creating delicious meals!

Tips and tricks

You don't need any special training to cook our recipes, only pleasure in cooking and a kitchen with standard equipment.

Thanks to the easily understood descriptions and step by step instructions, our recipes can even be cooked without problems by beginners in the culinary arts. And more experienced cooks will be sure to find all kinds of new ideas in the variations.

If there is anything special that should be noted, whether to do with the cooking of the meat or the preparation of the vegetables, we will draw your attention to it, so that nothing should go wrong.

Variations

The aim of this book is to offer you the best variations on preparing the different kinds of meat, so you can choose the widest possible range of

options. To do this, we have taken different approaches for the individual topics; because steaks are at their best just as steaks, for example, the variations will give the option of different garnishes that will compliment, but not essentially change, the steaks.

But it's a different case with, say pork medallions, for there are many delicious cooking options available here. So, in this case, you will find both marinated medallions and medallions baked with cheese, and also recipes prepared with sauces. You will soon grasp the principle!

In our view, some dishes can only be combined with particular side dishes, sauces and dips. We do draw attention to this. But it is, of course, entirely up to you to decide if you want to try out new taste experiences.

Quality of meat

Another note on the quality of meat: you need a good piece of meat to make a truly tasty meal. So when you buy poultry, beef, veal, or lamb, check on the producers.

Questions about the housing, feeding, and transport of the animals are a good indicator of quality. Animals raised in intensive farming conditions are subject to a great deal of stress in their lives, and are often protected by drugs such as antibiotics from diseases that can break out very quickly in a crowded environment. The residues of feed and drugs find their way into the meat, and are then absorbed into our own bodies.

INFO
ORGANIC MEAT

If you decide to buy organically raised meat, you can assume that these animals have not only been raised and kept in species-appropriate conditions, but are give organically cultivated feed and receive drugs only in emergencies. These advantages also show up in flavor and consistency. **Organic meat** will lose less liquid during frying and simply tastes better. This is definitely worth the slightly higher price.

Beef

The term "beef" in the trade, covers the meat of young bulls, steers, oxen, heifers, and cows. Young bulls are uncastrated males. They are slaughtered between the ages of 16 and 22 months.

Steers and oxen are castrated cattle, usually slaughtered between 20 and 30 months, as are heifers, the young female animals. Cows are older females, about 5 years old, but the meat is not as popular.

The meat of young steers and heifers is marbled, fine in texture and tender. Young bulls often have very lean, but less finely textured meat.

The meat of these young animals has a very aromatic flavor.

Nearly all parts of cattle are used as meat, with the most tender parts being the tenderloin, sirloin, and round.

Beef must be well hung and, according to the type of meat, can be fried, roasted, broiled, grilled, stewed, or braised.

If well packaged, beef will keep in the refrigerator for 3-4 days (roasts and cooked meat) or 2-3 days (steaks). The exception is ground beef, which should be used straight away. Provided the meat has not previously been frozen and thawed out, it can be stored in the freezer on the day of purchase.

Veal

Veal is the meat of young male cattle (calves), slaughtered at the age of 4 months when they reach a weight of 330 lb (150 kg). Milk calves are fed exclusively on milk for 8 weeks.

Veal is very low in fat and particularly tender, and also has a finer structure than beef.

The flavor is less marked than that of the meat of older animals.

Almost all parts of the calf are used for veal as well, with the fillet (from the back) and eye of round being the finest cuts. Meat from these cuts is particularly well suited to quick frying. Veal escalopes are cut from the round.

Breast of veal is also very juicy, and excellent for stuffing, roasting, and braising. The name is true shoulder of veal. The fore and hind shank—whole or sliced—can be braised or stewed.

Veal will keep fresh in the icebox for 2-3 days, and for 2 days more if cooked.

It can be stored in the freezer, provided it has not previously been frozen and allowed to thaw.

Pork

Pork comes from domesticated pigs and is very popular in the kitchen. The animals are slaughtered at the age of 6-7 months when they reach a weight of 260 lb (120 kg). Suckling pigs are 6 weeks old, and up to 33 lb (15 kg) in weight.

Pork tends to be fat marbled and has an aromatic flavor.

All parts of the pig are used in cooking—right down to the trotters.

Pork tenderloin, rib, and loin chops come from the back. Pork steaks come from the back, blade, and ham cuts. Cuts for roasts and escalopes are also cut from the ham section. Pork blade or Boston butt is slightly marbled with fat, but juicy. Boston butt is often used for roasting with crackling.

Pork can be fried, roasted, braised, broiled, and boiled.

It is important to cook the meat thoroughly.

Please keep the pork in the icebox, well wrapped. It can be stored in the freezer, provided it has not been previously frozen and thawed out.

Lamb

Lamb is the meat of a young sheep, about 9 months old. Spring lamb is from lambs that are 3-4 months old. The meat of animals up to 1 year old—whether female or (castrated) male—is known as yearling lamb, and that of older animals as mutton.

The meat of younger animals is tender and aromatic. As they age, the meat becomes tougher, fattier, and harsher in flavor. How the animals are fed and kept also influences the flavor of the meat.

Leg of lamb is very popular in cooking; this is the largest, and leanest, joint. Fillet and chops come

from the loin. Meat from the boneless shoulder, shoulder, and neck is also used, but it is less tender and therefore better suited to goulash and stews.

Lamb and yearling lamb can be fried, roasted, braised, broiled, or stewed. It is excellent for marinating and should always be eaten hot, as the fat hardens quickly.

Fresh lamb, properly packed, will keep for 3 days in the icebox. It can be stored in the freezer, provided it has not been previously frozen and allowed to thaw.

Poultry

Poultry generally covers domesticated fowl such as chicken (including poulade and capon), duck, goose, turkey, pigeon, quail, and guinea fowl, with chicken being the most popular by far.

Depending on the age and method of raising, poultry meat is particularly tender and aromatic in flavor. Chicken, turkey, pigeon, guinea fowl, and quail meat have less fat than duck or goose. Breast meat is paler and has less fat than leg meat, but is also drier.

Poultry is sold whole or in portions as breast fillet, leg or wing portions. Poultry offal, e.g. chicken liver, is also popular.

Chicken can be fried, roasted, braised, broiled, and stewed. It must always be well cooked, however, and never eaten rare. Whole poultry are

excellent for stuffing. Poultry meat cut small can be used in fricassées.

Raw poultry meat deteriorates quickly and should not be kept in the icebox for more than 1 day. It can be stored in the freezer provided it has not been previously frozen and thawed out.

Ground meat

Ground meat is made from beef, veal, pork, and lamb. Ground poultry meat is less common, though ground turkey and chicken is available.

To produce ground meat, pieces from the shoulder or breast are put through a mill. As this destroys the cell structure, ground meat is particularly susceptible to salmonella infection. It should therefore be cooked on the day you buy it. Even better, buy the meat cut into small pieces and put them through a meat grinder at home shortly before cooking.

Poultry meat should be cut small, with a very sharp knife, or put through a meat grinder at home, and then most definitely cooked at once.

Mixed ground meat is available, often composed of equal parts of pork and beef meat. Alternatively, you can buy ground pork and beef and make your own mix. As ground beef becomes very dry when fried or baked, the ground pork adds the extra fat required.

Ground meat is very versatile. It can be used for fillings, meatloaves, patties, hamburgers, and meat sauces. There are many baked dishes such as moussaka, in which ground beef is used.

Always cook ground meat thoroughly, and never keep it for more than 1 day in the fridge. Frozen, it will keep for 3-4 months.

COOKING METHODS

Quick-frying

In quick-frying, the meat is cooked in a frying pan for a relatively short period of time, depending on the desired degree of cooking.

Suitable meats are mainly slices of meat such as steaks (beef, pork) escalopes (pork, poultry), chops (pork, lamb), and fillet (pork, beef, lamb). Goujons of meat (as in Geschnetzeltes) and patties or meatballs can also be cooked in a skillet, though here it is important, as with poultry, to ensure they are thoroughly cooked.

Oils that can be heated to a high temperature, such as, for example, sunflower oil, are particularly suitable for quick-frying. Clarified butter is also suitable. There are also specially branded frying oils on the market.

How to do it: first heat the oil or clarified butter in a skillet to a high temperature (about 350 °F/180 °C). Then put the pieces of meat, previously washed and patted dry, into the pan and fry on both sides

over high heat, until brown all over. Now turn down the heat and finish cooking the meat until you achieve the desired degree of cooking.

Roasting in the oven

In roasting, meat is cooked in the oven with a little fat. This method is excellent for large joints of meat (see braising) and poultry.

You can put the joint of meat in a roasting pan or on a rack standing in a pan to catch the meat juices. You

can use the juices later to produce a sauce or gravy.

Another method is to roast the meat at a low temperature. It is then cooked at 120 °F/50 °C–140 °F/60 °C for 5-8 hours, according to size. This makes the meat especially tender and juicy.

How to do it: put the meat which you have previously washed, patted dry, and seasoned, in a roasting pan or wire rack. If using the rack, place the roasting tin underneath to catch the juices. Brush the meat with oil and then brown in the oven at 350 °F/180 °C or 400 °F/200 °C, then continue to roast at 275 °F/140 °C–325 °F/160 °C, until the meat is cooked to the desired degree. During roasting, brush or baste the meat with additional fat and the cooking juices, to prevent drying out.

Braising

In braising, larger pieces of pork, veal, beef, or lamb are first browned over high heat in fat and then cooked, covered, at a lower temperature in liquid until done.

Particularly suitable for braising are meat from the ham cut (pork), round and rump (veal, lamb) and eye of round (beef).

For braising, you should also use oils that can be heated to a high temperature, or clarified butter.

How to do it: first heat the oil or clarified butter in a roasting pan or casserole (to 350 °F/180 °C). Then add the piece of meat, which you have previously washed and patted dry, and fry over high heat on all sides until browned

Now pour over liquid according to the recipe and, if required, add

flavoring ingredients such as vegetables. Then cover the roasting pan or casserole, and cook for the required time (depending on the thickness and other features of the meat).

Poaching

In poaching, the pieces of meat are placed without fat, in liquid such as stock, water, or wine and cooked, as it were, in their own juices. This is the gentlest and healthiest method of cooking. Poaching is braising without frying the meat first.

The color structure, and flavor of the meat itself are best preserved in this cooking method.

Pale meat such as veal or poultry is suitable for poaching.

You can poach in the oven or on top of the stove.

How to do it: put the meat in a pan with seasoning, add a little liquid, bring to the boil, then reduce the heat, cover the pan, and simmer gently.

The time taken for the meat to cook will depend on its size.

Cooking with a topping

When cooking with a topping, the essential point is to give the meat that has already been cooked, such as escalopes or medallions, a crispy

crust—of cheese, for example, or a mixture of butter, seasoning, and/or nuts. You can bake with a topping in the oven or under the broiler.

How to do it: Take the mix for the topping you want (cheese, herbs, nuts, a mixture of seasoning, and/or breadcrumbs) and spread them on each piece of meat. Bake or broil until the cheese has melted and the crust is golden brown.

**INFO
QUANTITIES**

In this book you will find that the ingredients are always given in Imperial (American) measurements followed by the Metric equivalent. Please see page 2 for a conversion table and an explanation of the abbreviations.

Broiling and grilling

The difference between broiling and grilling is that, in the former method, the meat is cooked with the heat source above it, e.g. by placing it under the broiler, either on aluminum foil or a rack with a drip pan underneath. When meat is grilled, it is with the heat source underneath, e.g. on a rack over hardwood, charcoal, or gas in the summertime

If you don't want to barbecue or use the broiler, however, you can always cook the meat in a stove-top grill. It does not need any fat, and gives the meat the typical "grilled" stripes. The flavor, however, is not really comparable to that of properly grilled or broiled meat.

Steaks (beef, pork, lamb), chops (pork, lamb) and poultry portions such as leg joints or drumsticks are especially good for grilling and broiling. The lass fat the meat has, however, the more it needs to be marinated before cooking.

How to do it: before grilling or broiling, brush the meat well with a marinade or oil, to prevent it from drying out. If the meat has a border of fat, make cuts in it to stop the meat curling during cooking.

Now put it on the barbecue or under the broiler and cook for the time specified in the recipe. During cooking, brush the meat repeatedly with marinade or oil, and take care not to let anything burn.

Sauces and dips

For many recipes and variations in this cookbook, we recommend sauces and dips. In these recommendations, we limit ourselves to the ingredients without quantities, so you need a bit of cooking experience.
Here are a few tips to creating a perfect sauce:

Sauces can be made in several different ways; in roasting, the meat juices can be collected and made into a gravy with water, bouillon, or wine.

If the meat is marinated, the marinade can be added during cooking. It can also be used to make a sauce.

Gravy can be thickened with light or heavy cream, sour cream, yogurt, crème fraîche, whipping cream, or clarified butter. Tomato purée can also be added. You can also give the sauce a spicy or fresh flavor with chopped herbs or spices.

(mustard, horseradish, lemon juice, etc.) is then added.

If you are using a method where there are no meat juices, for example, broiling or quick-frying, but you still want to serve a sauce with it, we recommend a dip. Of course, to make sure there's something for everyone, you could prepare several dips for the same meal. As an alternative, you can fall back on sauces frozen in portions (there is often some left over and it's a pity to throw it away).

It is possible to thicken sauces in several different ways.

The classic way is to use starch, generally corn or potato starch, or flour, which is mixed with a little water and then stirred into the sauce to thicken it when brought to the boil.

Flour and butter are combined to thicken sauces as follows: knead equal amounts of flour and cold butter

It takes a little longer to boil down or, as the professionals say, "reduce" the sauce. This does give the sauce the best taste and aroma, as the flavors of the ingredients become concentrated during reduction. Tomato sauce that has been reduced after several hours cooking time tastes truly wonderful.

Reduced meat gravies can be bound with flakes of ice-cold butter. Beat the butter together with the gravy, and serve at once—before the butter and sauce separate again.

For thickening with egg yolk, the egg yolk is beated with a little milk, cream, or meat juices until smooth, and then added to the hot sauce. It is important not to let the sauce boil, as the egg yolk will curdle.

In choosing the ingredients for a sauce, there need be no limits to your imagination. Even unusual ingredients, such as Fanta®, Coca-Cola®, coffee, or melted chocolate can be tasty. In the right quantity, they can add that final kick to a sauce.

If the meat is stewed or poached, an additional sauce, for example, horseradish or mustard sauce is usually served. These are usually based on a roux, where flour is stirred into melted butter, stock is poured over, and the actual flavoring

together, and add it bit by bit to the boiling sauce, stirring all the time.

If pieces of vegetable, potato, or fruit are cooked with the sauce, they can be puréed after cooking to make the sauce creamy.

Side dishes

We have tried to keep a balance in choosing the side dishes. We recommend potatoes cooked in all kinds of ways—from French fries, through dumplings, to gratins—and also many different versions of rice, sometimes with herbs and vegetables and sometimes with fruit, and pasta from fusilli through tagliatelle. But we also include grain-based side dishes, such as polenta, bulgur, and couscous.

Where, in our opinion, none of these filling side dishes would taste right, you will find a recipe for bread, or one for croutons.

Other side dishes, of course, include all kinds of vegetables, fresh or frozen, braised, sautéed, boiled, baked with a topping, raw in a salad, fresh or dried, and mixtures of the above, or of vegetables and fruit. Here, too, all you

Herbs and spices

For every dish, it is the herbs and spices that add the final touch. They emphasize or complement the flavors of the vegetables, meat, or fish with their specific aromas while at the same time being good for your health. Many of them are good for digestion.

The rule is: the fresher the better. Popular kitchen herbs are parsley, chives, dill, fennel, chervil, tarragon, lovage, marjoram, thyme, oregano, sage, cilantro, and basil.

One of more of them is an ingredient in almost every recipe. Fresh herbs have to be finely chopped; usually, the leaves must first be removed from their hard stems or stalks. Only chives can be cut right away. You can, of course, also use dried herbs.

Spices and seasonings can be bought ready ground. It is not unusual, though, for the aroma and flavor to suffer as a result. If possible, should grind salt and pepper freshly with a mill, and grate whole nutmeg.

Here too, we have not given any quantities, as these side dishes are merely meant to be suggestions for you. Here is a tip, however: with potatoes, plan for about 1³/₄ lb-2¹/₄ lb (800 g-1 kg); for pasta, 14 oz (400 g), and for rice polenta, bulgar, and couscous, about 1¹/₄ cups (250 g)—quantities for 4 servings. For the rest, you can experiment here, too, and decide whether you prefer to add 1 or 2 onions, 2 or 3 bell peppers, 3¹/₂ or 5¹/₂ oz (100 or 150 g) mushrooms to the rice, couscous, or pasta, or 5 or 7 tablespoons of grated Parmesan to the polenta.

need to do is follow your own taste. You can also find delicious vegetable recipes in the Vegetable Variations Cookbook part of this series.

Preparation

In order to be able to offer you more recipes, we have for reasons of space left out some instructions from the step by step descriptions of the method. These instructions actually apply in all cases and are listed here.

If you use unpeeled vegetables, always wash them well beforehand, best of all in hot water. Always wash lettuce as well, preferably before shredding, otherwise you will lose too many nutrients. If you have used organic vegetables, you can re-use the water they were cooked in.

Unless otherwise specified, peel onions and garlic before use;

Peel carrots, or scrub them with a brush;

Peel and pit avocados and mangoes; peel pineapples.

Clean mushrooms, removing any remaining compost with a brush and wiping the caps with a damp cloth (do not wash mushrooms as they soak up water);

Use citrus fruit with unwaxed peel; and the best of all, buy organic fruit.

Tips and tricks

Meat will cook more quickly if it is at room temperature before the start of cooking.

If a piece of meat releases too much liquid at the start of frying or roasting, the starting temperature is too low and the meat will dry out.

Quick-fried meat should only be seasoned with salt and pepper after frying.

After frying or roasting, all pieces of meat (except for meat that has been breaded) and joints should be wrapped in aluminum foil and allowed to rest for 10-15 minutes in a very low oven (120 °F/50 °C).

If you want to be sure that your roast is thoroughly cooked, it is best to use a meat thermometer, which you stick into the joint. It will show

the internal temperature of the joint and indicate when it is cooked right through.

Kitchen equipment

As we have already said, you do not need a specially equipped kitchen to cook these recipes.

You should have a standard stove, whether it is gas, electric, has a ceramic glass hob, or an induction hob.

For roasting and baking, you require an oven.

You can use the broiler to broil and to melt and crisp toppings. Of course, for proper grilling, a barbecue (charcoal, gas, electric, or hardwood) is best. But even on a stove-top grill, meat will get that typical grill pattern.

Also very useful for blending, stirring, and chopping are a food processor, blender, and electric handheld blender.

An electric grinder could also be useful; for example, for grinding meat,

potatoes, or vegetables if you use large quantities.

In order to provide a complete list, we mention some of the more unusual kitchen equipment—you can decide if you need it in your kitchen.

A special table-top broiler is useful for baking toppings and melting cheese.

There are specialized cookers for preparing rice—they are useful, because the rice in them is cooked to perfection, but are only worthwhile if you eat a lot of rice.

Then there are steamers for particularly gentle cooking without fat, and the so-called slow cookers or crock pots. These are electric pots in which meals are slowly stewed or braised. They are useful if you go out to work; you put the food in the crock pot in the morning and it cooks

all day at a very slow heat. By the evening, your meal is ready. That doesn't just save on electricity, it also preserves vitamins.

Kitchen utensils

To cook these meals you need pans; at least 1 small, 1 medium, and 1 large pan. A large, ovenproof dish is also required.

You will also need a casserole or roasting pan that will hold a joint big enough for 4 people, or a similar sized duck, goose, or chicken.

1-2 skillets are a good idea. Aluminum or cast iron pans with a non-scratch coating are best. A small copper pan for melting butter would be a good idea.

For sieving and draining, you need several sizes of sieve, and perhaps a food mill to purée sauces and vegetables.

Sharp knives are essential; large ones for meat and vegetables, smaller ones for slicing potatoes, for example, You will also need peelers for vegetables and fruit, a serrated knife for chopping onions and herbs, a garlic press, a vegetable slicer or mandoline for thinly sliced cucumber, julienne carrots etc., and a grater for vegetables and cheese. A small nutmeg grater is very handy too. To protect your working surfaces, you should have 1-2 wood or plastic chopping boards (reserve one for meat only).

Other useful aids in the kitchen include a potato ricer, a rolling pin, a slotted spoon, wooden spoons, whisk, measuring cups, and jugs, bowls in various sizes in metal or plastic—and don't forget the kitchen scales.

QUICK-FRIED MEAT

Quick-fried meat dishes are tasty treats that do not need much work.

Try a classic top round steak or escalope, succulent lamb chops, chicken breasts for a lighter meal, or grilled meat skewers.

The range of different types of meat is huge—and so is the range of recipe options!

In this chapter, you will find all you need for many complete meals, including suggestions for complementary side dishes and sauces.

MEDIUM STEAK
with herb butter and lemon

Serves 4

1	*garlic clove, crushed*
4 tbsp	*finely chopped mixed herbs*
A few drops	*lemon juice*
6 tbsp	*butter*
	Salt
	Pepper
4–6 tbsp	*oil for frying*
4	*top round or sirloin steaks,*
	about 1 in. (2.4 cm) thick and 7 oz (200 g) in weight
4	*slices lemon*
A few	*parsley leaves*

Step by step

Mix the garlic with the herbs, lemon juice, and 4 tablespoons of softened butter. Season with salt and pepper.

Remove the steaks from the skillet, wrap in aluminum foil, and set aside for 2 minutes.

Heat 2–3 tablespoons of oil in a skillet, add the steaks, and fry over high heat for about 1 minute on each side. Reduce the heat and fry for a further minute on each side.

Unwrap the steaks and fry for a further 30 seconds on each side.

Add 1 tablespoon of butter. Melt over a lowered heat, coat the steaks, and continue frying for 1 minute on each side. Add seasoning to taste.

Place a slice of lemon on each steak, dot with herb butter, and garnish with parsley.

STEAK INFO

Still pink in the middle, but beautifully brown and crispy on the outside: that's how most people like their **steaks**. It is important to keep to the frying times, however, because even a minute will make a big difference. Serving it very rare, rare, medium, or well done is a matter of taste.

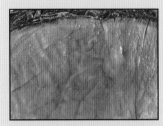

Very rare (1 min. each side) has a thin brown crust with a raw-looking center.

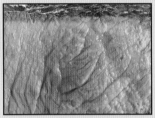

Rare (2 min. each side) is still deep red in the center, but the meat around it is pink.

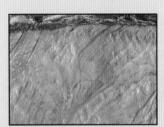

Medium (3 min. each side) means the steak will still be pink inside, but well browned on the outside.

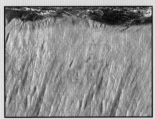

Well done (4–5 min. each side) is how we describe a steak cooked all the way through.

The frying times are guidelines for a 1-in. (2.4-cm) thick steak.

STEAKS

several variations

Top round or sirloin is the basic steak for all these variations, prepared as on the previous page (but without the herb butter). You can use the following suggestions to refine your steak recipes and create completely individual meals with minimal effort. You can, of course, use the same procedure for all cooking stages from very rare to well done—however you like it.

... with tomatoes, parsley, and chile

Skin a tomato, halve it, remove the seeds, and cut into eight pieces. Strip the leaves from a bunch of parsley, chop, then sweat for about 1 minute with $1/4$ finely chopped chile pepper in 2–3 tablespoons oil. Season with salt. Swirl the tomato pieces around in 3 teaspoons melted butter and distribute over the steaks, together with the parsley.

... with pears, Gorgonzola, and cranberries

Spread 4–5 oz (120–150 g) Gorgonzola on 4 canned pear halves. Dot with cranberry sauce. Bake in the oven for 4–5 minutes at 400 °F/200 °C. Serve the steaks topped with the pears.

... with bacon, sweet corn, and watercress

Heat 1–2 tablespoons oil in a skillet. Add 4 rashers of bacon and fry until crisp. Put a bacon rasher on each steak, then finish with a handful of chopped watercress and 1 tablespoon steamed sweet corn.

... with paprika, onions, and chives

Mix 1 tablespoon flour with 1 tablespoon paprika. Slice 4 onions into rings and coat with the flour and paprika mixture. Heat 3–4 tablespoons oil and fry the onion rings until crisp. Serve on the steaks with coarsely chopped chives.

SAUCES
for steak

These sauces are mainly just for steak, but can be used with the recipe variations if desired.

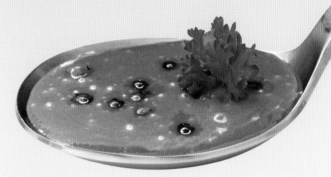

Pepper sauce

Mix the pan juices with a little butter, plenty of lightly crushed green peppercorns, and crème fraîche, then heat—the classic sauce for steak!

Mushroom and cream sauce

Sweat thinly sliced mushrooms and chopped scallions in the pan juices with a little butter and thyme until soft. Add some white wine and bouillon and bring to a boil, scraping up any meat pieces. Add 3 tablespoons light cream and simmer gently for 2 minutes.

Marsala sauce

Add some Marsala to the pan juices and reduce. Season to taste with lemon juice, salt, and pepper. Add ice-cold slivers of butter to bind the sauce.

... with mango and pomegranate

Peel and pit a mango, and cut the flesh into thick strips. Sweat in 1 tablespoon butter, together with the seeds of 1 pomegranate. Spread on the steaks and garnish with a few mint leaves.

... with peaches, Roquefort, and Armagnac

Crumble 3$\frac{1}{2}$ oz (100 g) Roquefort and mix to a creamy consistency with 1 tablespoon butter, 4 tablespoons light cream, 2 tablespoons Armagnac, and a little pepper. Sweat 4 canned peach halves in the pan juices, fill with the Roquefort mixture, and bake until the cheese is slightly runny.

ESCALOPE INFO

The traditional **Wiener Schnitzel** can only be called by this name if it is a veal escalope, because the name is protected. If, however, you are offered a "Schnitzel Wiener Art," the escalope will be pork, which is more economical. The original also has another distinguishing feature: it is beaten until very thin. A perfect Wiener Schnitzel is at most ¼ in. (6 mm) thick. Slices or wedges of

lemon are essential for a genuine Wiener Schnitzel.

ANCHOVY INFO

Anchovies belong to the herring family. They are small, slender fish, growing no longer than 8 in. (20 cm), and mostly no more than 6 in. (15 cm). The flesh of these oil-rich fish has a bitter flavor and is therefore

usually salted for cooking. This not only preserves the fish, but also causes them to ferment, almost as if they have been cooked. The storage time, which can be over two years, improves their quality and flavor. Anchovies are mainly sold as fillets in coarse sea salt, ordinary salt, or vegetable oil. Soaking in milk or lukewarm water makes the flavor milder. Puréed and mixed with oil and spices, they are sold in tubes as anchovy paste.

Serves 4

4	veal escalopes, about 6 oz (175 g) each
	Salt
2	eggs
²/₃ cup (100 g)	all-purpose flour
generous 1 cup (150 g)	dried breadcrumbs
1 cup (250 ml)	oil or clarified butter
1	lemon, cut into quarters
4	anchovies
	Parsley leaves

Step by step

Pat the escalopes dry, beat until flat, and season lightly with salt.

Heat the oil or clarified butter in a large skillet. Arrange the escalopes so that they float freely in the hot fat.

Beat the eggs in a shallow bowl. Pour the flour and the breadcrumbs onto two separate plates.

Fry the escalopes on both sides, 4 minutes a side, until golden brown. Shake the skillet frequently to allow the escalopes to cook evenly.

Flour the escalopes, dip them in the beaten egg, drain well, and coat them in the breadcrumbs. Press the coating well into the meat.

Drain the escalopes on paper towels. Garnish with lemon wedges, anchovies, and parsley leaves.

BREADED ESCALOPES—WIENER SCHNITZEL
with lemon, anchovies, and parsley

SIDE DISHES
for escalopes

Menu essentials for any traditional restaurant: these two side dishes will make classic escalope dishes taste perfect.

Potato salad

Boil 1³/₄ lb (800 g) medium-sized potatoes in their skins until soft, then peel and slice. Fold in 1 red bell pepper, cut into strips. Combine 3 tablespoons mayonnaise, 2 tablespoons lemon juice, 1 chopped onion, salt, pepper, and paprika to make a dressing and stir into the salad. Sprinkle with chopped parsley and chives.

Mixed bell peppers

Cut green and yellow bell peppers into strips, and peel and slice an onion. Sweat the vegetables in a frying pan for 3 minutes in 2 tablespoons butter. Add 7 tablespoons (100 ml) white wine. Season with salt, pepper, and sweet paprika.

... with Emmental, garlic, and sage

For the coating, mix ¹/₂ cup (50 g) dried breadcrumbs with 3¹/₂ oz (100 g) grated Emmental or other flavorful cheese, 1 crushed garlic clove, and 1 tablespoon crumbled, dried sage. Coat the escalopes in flour, egg, and breadcrumbs. Press the breadcrumb mixture firmly onto the meat and fry the escalopes for 4 minutes each side.

... with flour, egg, and coriander

This escalope is prepared in the same way as a Wiener Schnitzel, but not coated in breadcrumbs. Mix ²/₃ cup (100 g) all-purpose flour and 1 teaspoon ground coriander on a plate. Beat two eggs in a shallow bowl. Coat the escalopes in the flour mixture and dip in the egg. Drain well before frying for 4 minutes on each side.

BREADED ESCALOPES
s e v e r a l   v a r i a t i o n s

It doesn't always have to be the traditional breadcrumb coating such as that used for Wiener Schnitzel. In gourmet kitchens, freshly grated, stale, white bread is often used instead of packaged breadcrumbs, but there are plenty of other flavors to explore. In these recipes, you can choose whether to use veal or pork escalopes.

... with nuts and parsley

For the coating, mix generous 1 cup (150 g) ground filberts, 1 teaspoon sweet paprika, and 1 tablespoon chopped parsley together on a plate. Coat the escalopes in flour, then in beaten egg, and finally in the nut mixture. Press the coating firmly onto the escalopes and fry them for 4 minutes each side.

... with cornflakes and walnuts

This coating will give the escalopes a crunchy crust. Crush 3$^1/_2$ oz (100 g) unsweetened cornflakes with 1 heaped tablespoon ground walnuts. Mix the flour with 1 tablespoon marjoram. Coat the escalopes in the flour, then in beaten egg, and finally in the cornflake mixture. Press the coating firmly into the escalopes and fry for 4 minutes on each side.

... with sesame seeds, sweet paprika, and cilantro

For the coating, mix 3$^1/_2$ oz (100 g) sesame seeds with 1 teaspoon ground cumin and 1 teaspoon sweet paprika and put on a plate. Coat the escalopes in flour first, then in beaten egg, and finally in the sesame mixture. Press the coating firmly into the escalopes and fry for 4 minutes on each side. Garnish with fresh cilantro leaves.

... with tarragon, thyme, and mustard

For the coating, mix 1$^1/_2$ cups (150 g) dried breadcrumbs with 1 teaspoon tarragon and 1 teaspoon thyme. Beat the egg with 1 tablespoon medium-hot mustard in a shallow bowl. Coat the escalope in flour, then the egg mixture, and finally the breadcrumbs. Press the coating firmly into the escalopes and fry for 4 minutes on each side.

STUFFED ESCALOPES—CORDON BLEU
with ham, Emmental, and parsley

INFO

Mayonnaise is based on an emulsion of egg yolk and oil, to which you can add ingredients of your choice: for example, acidic flavors such as vinegar or lemon juice. But other flavors such as spices, mustard, ketchup, or sherry are also suitable for mayonnaise. You can use cream to increase the amount—or, if you want a lighter version, plain yogurt. Try it yourself: mayonnaise is nowhere near as difficult to make as you might think!

Serves 4

4	veal or pork escalopes, each about 6 oz (175 g): (ask the butcher to cut a pocket in each one)
	Salt
	Pepper
¹/₂	bunch parsley, finely chopped
2 thick	slices cooked ham, 1¾ oz (50 g) each, halved
2 thick	slices Emmental, 1¾ oz (50 g) each, halved
	Toothpicks
2 tbsp	all-purpose flour
scant cup (80 g)	dried breadcrumbs
1	egg
6 tbsp	oil or clarified butter
1	unwaxed lemon, cut into quarters

Step by step

Pat the escalopes dry and season inside and out with salt and pepper.

Stuff the pockets with parsley, half a ham slice, and half a cheese slice. Use the toothpicks to close the pockets.

Put flour on one plate, and breadcrumbs on another. Beat an egg in a bowl and season with salt and pepper.

Coat the escalopes in the flour, then the egg, and finally the breadcrumbs. Press the coating on firmly.

Fry the breaded escalopes in hot fat for 4 minutes each side over medium heat. Serve with lemon wedges.

Side dish

Potatoes au gratin taste wonderful served with a cordon bleu escalope. To make, wash 1¹/₄ lb (800 g) potatoes, peel them, and slice very thinly. Layer the potato slices in a greased baking pan and season each layer with salt and pepper. Mix 1 cup (250 ml) milk and 1 cup (250 ml) light cream and season with salt, pepper, and nutmeg. Pour over the potatoes. Sprinkle with 3¹/₂ oz (100 g) grated Emmental and bake in the oven for about 40 minutes at 350 °F/180 °C.

Salad

For a vitamin boost to go with your escalopes: **Carrot salad with orange dressing.** To make, peel generous 1 lb (500 g) carrots and grate them finely. Mix 3 teaspoons fresh orange juice, 1 teaspoon sugar, a little salt, and 3 tablespoons oil, stir into the carrots—and the salad is ready!

SIDE DISHES
for escalopes

These three vegetable side dishes are simply delicious with escalopes:

Cauliflower au gratin
Put 14 oz (400 g) cauliflower florets cooked al dente in a baking pan. Sprinkle with a mixture of $^2/_3$ cup (100 g) each all-purpose flour and grated Parmesan. Bake for 15 minutes at 350 °F/180 °C. Suitable for all fillings.

Sliced carrots in butter
Stir 3 tablespoons butter into 14 oz (400 g) hot, sliced carrots, cooked al dente. Season with salt and serve with thyme. Suitable for the Swiss chard and mushroom filling.

Broccoli with almonds
Cook 14 oz (400 g) broccoli florets in salted water until al dente, then season with salt, pepper, and nutmeg. Mix with slivered almonds toasted in a skillet. Suitable for all fillings.

STUFFED ESCALOPES
several

Escalopes—whether veal, beef, pork, or turkey—are ideal for stuffing. Best of all, when you buy them, you can ask your butcher to cut a pocket for the filling. This makes them much easier to prepare. Here are some recipes to surprise your guests!

... with bacon, prunes, and Madeira
Fill each pocket with 2 rashers lightly fried bacon, 2 halved and pitted prunes, and 1 tablespoon Madeira. Season. Close the pockets, coat the escalopes, and fry.

... with boiled ham, Butterkäse, and spinach
Blanch 7 oz (200 g) spinach, drain thoroughly, then chop and season with salt, pepper, and nutmeg. Divide the spinach between the 4 pockets, then add 1 slice Butterkäse and 1 slice boiled ham to each. Close the pockets, coat the escalopes, and fry.

...ariations

Along with the classic cordon bleu on the previous page, there are plenty of other fillings for escalopes to choose from. Surprise your guests! As to the coating, the choice is yours.

... with Swiss chard and mushrooms

Lightly blanch 4 leaves of Swiss chard. Combine 1¾ oz (50 g) chopped mushrooms with 1¾ oz (50 g) diced bacon and fry in a little oil. Put 1 chard leaf in each pocket with ¼ of the mushroom mixture. Season. Close the pockets, coat the escalopes, and fry.

... with leeks and bread

Dice 3½ oz (100 g) bacon and ½ an onion. Thinly slice a small leek. Sauté together for about 5 minutes in 1 tablespoon clarified butter. Stir in 1 crumbled bread roll and 1 egg yolk. Season with salt, pepper, and oregano then divide the mixture between the pockets. Close the pockets, coat the escalopes, and fry.

SAUCES
for escalopes

Delicious flavors inside and out: discover which sauce goes best with which filling.

Tartare sauce

Improve a rémoulade sauce with a chopped, hard-boiled egg and finely diced onion. A good accompaniment for cordon bleu and leek stuffed escalopes.

Cocktail sauce

Mix ketchup and mayonnaise together. Refine with a little brandy to taste. Sprinkle with freshly ground pepper.

Rémoulade sauce

Beat an egg yolk together with salt, pepper, sugar, vinegar, and mustard. Slowly stir oil into the mixture. Combine with chopped gherkins and parsley, plus some capers. A good accompaniment to cordon bleu and leek filled escalopes, but also goes well with the boiled ham, Butterkäse, and spinach stuffing.

PORK CHOPS

with paprika, tomatoes, and onions

Serves 4

4	pork chops, about 7 oz (200 g) each
	Salt
	Flour for coating
3 tbsp	oil or clarified butter
¹/₂ cup (125 ml)	beef bouillon
1	onion, sliced into rings
1	crushed garlic clove
2 tbsp (30 g)	Butter
1	red bell pepper, cut into strips
1	green bell pepper, cut into strips
3	tomatoes, cut into quarters
	Paprika
	Slices of cucumber and salad leaves to garnish

Step by step

Beat the chops to flatten them slightly, make a cut along the bone, season with salt, turn the beaten side in flour, and dust off the excess.

Add the chops, turn several times, and remove from the pan.

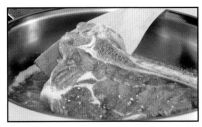

Heat the fat in a pan, brown the floured side of the meat over high heat, and turn briefly. Wrap in aluminum foil and keep warm.

Sweat the onions and garlic in a little butter, add the bell peppers and tomatoes, and season with salt and paprika.

Drain the fat from the pan, add the beef bouillon, and bring to a boil, scraping up the meat pieces stuck to the pan.

Put the chops on top and braise for 15 minutes. Garnish with cucumber and salad leaves.

CHOPS INFO

Chops are finger-thick slices of meat on the bone and can be veal, pork, lamb, mutton, or game. Beef can be had as a cutlet. Here we have a few suggestions for recipes using pork chops. And because the most varied kinds of meat go well together, you can find the corresponding recipes for lamb chops from page 38 onward. Chops are distinguished by their origin from different parts of the animal: loin, rib, and blade chops are all part of the rib section.

The back section, known as the **loin**, is also boned and cut into pork steaks.

The meat on the **rib chops** is very delicate; when fried, it can become a little dry.

Blade chops are well marbled, making them especially juicy.

33

QUICK-FRIED MEAT

SALADS
for chops

Make these salads with Feta, wild herbs, and bell peppers and they will go beautifully with pork chops.

Feta salad
Simply mix green bell peppers cut into strips, onion rings, diced Feta, and thinly sliced cucumber with coarsely ground pepper, vinegar, and oil.

Wild herb salad
Cut young dandelion and sorrel leaves into strips and add some watercress. Toss in a mixture of oil, vinegar, a little salt, pepper, and finely chopped chervil.

Mixed bell pepper salad
Cut red and green bell peppers into very thin strips and slice some onions into rings. Toss in a dressing of lemon juice, salt, sugar, and oil.

... with caraway and garlic
Fry the chops, remove from the pan, and keep warm. Lightly brown 2 crushed garlic cloves in the pan juices, add 1 cup bouillon or veal stock, then add $^1/_2$ teaspoon caraway seeds and bind the sauce with 2–3 tablespoons ice-cold butter. Serve the sauce with the chops.

... with tomatoes, capers, and basil
Rub the chops with garlic and olive oil, fry until golden brown, and remove from the pan. Add the juice of 1 lemon to the pan juices, then quickly heat a mixture of $1^1/_2$ lb (700 g) skinned and diced beefsteak tomatoes, 1 tablespoon crushed capers, 2 teaspoons chopped basil, 1 tablespoon balsamic vinegar, 2 tablespoons olive oil, salt, and pepper in the pan, and pour around the chops.

PORK CHOPS
several variations

Here are six different variations for fried pork chops, covering a wide range of flavors. The recipes range from the fresh, light taste of lemon through the strong and spicy flavors of garlic and caraway. For chops with a sauce that are finished in the oven, the frying time is reduced by 5 minutes.

... with lemon sauce

Drizzle the chops with the juice of $^1/_2$ lemon and fry on each side until golden brown. Season with salt and pepper, remove from the pan, and keep warm. Drain the oil from the pan, retaining the meat juices. Add the juice of $^1/_2$ lemon to the pan and reduce a little. Add 2 tablespoons butter and 1 teaspoon grated lemon rind, and season to taste.

... with mushrooms, parsley, and crème fraîche

Melt 2 tablespoons butter in the chop pan. Lightly fry 9 oz (250 g) thinly sliced mushrooms for 3 minutes, season with salt and pepper, and sprinkle with a little chopped parsley. Stir in 2 tablespoons crème fraîche. Serve the sauce with the chops.

... with eggs, anchovies, and caper berries

Rub 4 chops with pepper. Fry until golden brown in 1 tablespoon butter, season with salt, remove from the pan, and keep warm. In a second pan, heat 1 tablespoon butter. Fry 4 sunny-side-up eggs in the butter and season with salt and pepper. Serve the chops on individual plates, with a fried egg and 1 rolled anchovy fillet. Sprinkle with 1–2 tablespoons chopped caper berries.

... with pineapple, boiled ham, and curry powder

Rub the chops with salt, pepper, and curry powder, then fry. Brown 4 slices of canned pineapple, halved, in the meat juices and sprinkle lightly with curry powder. Add a little pineapple juice, reduce a little, and stir in 1 tablespoon chopped sage. Top each chop with $^1/_2$ slice boiled ham and $^1/_2$ slice pineapple. Drizzle with the pineapple sauce, sprinkle with $3^1/_2$ oz (100 g) grated Gouda cheese, and bake until the cheese has melted.

SAMPHIRE INFO

Marsh samphire is a perennial herb with succulent, bright green leaves, a member of the amaranth family, which can grow to a height of 18 in. (45 cm). To flourish, this edible, wild plant requires salt. It is therefore found in marshy areas where land has been won back from the sea. When growing, the plant takes salt from the ground, thus "cleansing" it. A gourmet name for marsh samphire is sea asparagus. Only the young plants, and indeed only the tips of these, are really tasty. They are harvested from May onward. As the plant ages, it becomes woody. Samphire is rich in minerals and naturally

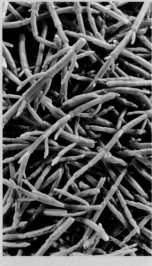

contains plenty of high-quality iodine. The flavor is spicy and slightly peppery.
Marsh samphire can be found in well-stocked delicatessens or specialty fisheries. The price is higher than that of "real" asparagus.
To prepare, blanch briefly in boiling water, pour off the liquid, and drain well. While still hot, stir in some butter, add a few skinned, pitted, and diced tomatoes, and serve—a healthy and delicious side dish. Young samphire plants can also be eaten raw.

Serves 4

1	rack of lamb 1¾ lb (800 g)
½ tsp	chile powder or flakes
3 tbsp	olive oil for the marinade
	Salt
	Pepper
1 tsp	thyme
1 tsp	lemon juice
1 tbsp	honey
1 tbsp	olive oil for frying
Tip	Use a whole rack of lamb for this recipe and only divide it into individual cutlets after cooking. This will keep the meat tender and juicy.

Step by step

Cut the rack of lamb into two pieces and pat dry with paper towels.

Marinade for 2 hours, wrapped in plastic wrap. Then remove the wrap.

For the marinade, mix the chile with the olive oil, salt, and pepper. Add the thyme, lemon juice, and honey.

Fry over high heat for 2–3 minutes in olive oil. Finish cooking in the oven for 8–10 minutes at 275 °F/140 °C, brushed with the marinade.

Baste the pieces of meat on both sides with the marinade.

Remove the pieces of meat from the baking pan and cut into 4 chops.

LAMB CHOPS
with chile and honey marinade

LAMB CHOPS
several variations

Lamb has a tasty, distinctive flavor, and yet is very tender. Just the thing for special or festive occasions. Lamb is ideal—not just for frying and roasting, but also for grilling.

... with whiskey, ginger, and mint marinade

Stir 2 tablespoons whiskey, plus some pepper and ground ginger, 2 chopped garlic cloves, and 2 tablespoons chopped mint into 3 tablespoons oil. Marinate the meat for 2 hours, then pat dry. Grill on both sides for 6–8 minutes. Heat the marinade, stir in 4 tablespoons light cream, and season to taste. Cut the rack of lamb into chops, season with salt, and serve with the cream sauce.

... with garlic, rosemary, and sage

Heat 2 tablespoons olive oil and 2 tablespoons butter. Slice 4 cloves garlic and sweat for 10 minutes in the fat with 1 teaspoon rosemary and 6 sage leaves. Remove the herbs and garlic. Fry the rack of lamb over high heat for about 3 minutes each side. Cut into chops, season with salt and pepper, and serve with herbs.

... with lemon balm butter and scallions

Marinate the rack of lamb in 3 tablespoons lemon juice, 1 chopped clove garlic, 1 teaspoon sage, and some pepper. Stir 3 tablespoons chopped lemon balm into 3$\frac{1}{2}$ tablespoons (50 g) butter with 1 tablespoon lemon juice, salt, and pepper. Lightly sauté 1 bunch chopped scallions in 1 tablespoon butter and season with salt. Fry the rack of lamb (see above), cut into chops, and serve with lemon balm butter and scallions.

... with peaches, mozzarella, and oregano

Marinate the rack of lamb for 2 hours in 3 tablespoons oil with 1 chopped garlic clove and $\frac{1}{2}$ tablespoon each chopped marjoram and thyme, plus 1 teaspoon grated lemon peel. Then fry (see above) and cut into chops. Cover with 12 peach wedges, season with salt and pepper, and sprinkle with 3 tablespoons chopped oregano. Cover with 4$\frac{1}{2}$ oz (125 g) mozzarella slices, and bake until the cheese has melted.

SIDE DISHES
for lamb chops

Because rosemary is the perfect accompaniment for lamb, rosemary potatoes top the list of side dishes. A medley of spring vegetables rounds off the meal.

... with kiwi, apricot, and curry powder

Fry the rack of lamb for 3 minutes each side in 3 tablespoons olive oil. Keep warm. Sauté 3 chopped garlic cloves and 1 teaspoon curry powder in the meat juices. Peel and dice 1 kiwi and 1 apricot and add to the garlic and curry powder. Add 1$^1/_2$ cups (350 ml) light cream and a pinch of cinnamon, and cook until the sauce thickens. Cut the rack of lamb into chops, season with salt, and pour over the sauce to serve.

Rosemary potatoes

Cut unpeeled potatoes in half lengthways, sprinkle the cut surface with salt and rosemary, and drizzle with a little oil. Bake in the oven on a greased baking sheet, cut side uppermost, for 30–40 minutes at 400 °F/200 °C.

... with tomatoes, zucchini, and olives

Rub the rack of lamb with pepper. Fry in 3 tablespoons olive oil (see above), and keep warm. Chop 1 onion and 1 garlic glove and brown in the meat juices with $^1/_2$ teaspoon rosemary, 7 oz (200 g) diced tomatoes, 4$^1/_2$ oz (125 g) sliced zucchini, and 1$^3/_4$ oz (50 g) halved black olives, then add a little water and simmer for 10–15 minutes. Season the rack of lamb with salt, cut into chops, and pour over the sauce to serve.

Mixed vegetables

Roughly chop some broccoli, asparagus, scallions, and cherry tomatoes. Cook the asparagus and broccoli in a pan of salt water until al dente, drain, and rinse with ice water. Briefly sweat the scallions and tomatoes in butter. Add a little balsamic vinegar and the rest of the vegetables, mix, and season with salt and pepper.

PORK MEDALLIONS
with bacon and mushrooms

Serves 4

1³/₄ lb (800 g)	pork tenderloin
6	rashers bacon, halved
	Salt and pepper
3 tbsp	rosemary leaves, chopped
4 tbsp	oil
7 oz (200 g)	mushrooms
2 tbsp	butter
2 tbsp	white wine
7 tbsp (100 ml)	meat bouillon

Step by step

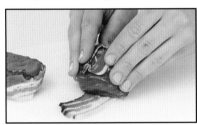

Cut the pork tenderloin into 12 medallions of equal size, press them flat, and wrap each one in a half rasher of bacon.

Clean the mushrooms, dry with a damp cloth, and cut into thin slices.

Season the medallions on both sides with salt and pepper, and sprinkle with chopped rosemary.

Heat the butter in a pan, add the mushrooms, and cook for 3 minutes, stirring.

Fry the medallions in 4 tablespoons oil for 1 minute each side. Reduce the heat and cook for another 3 minutes. Keep warm.

Pour in the wine and the bouillon. Allow the sauce to reduce a little.

POLENTA INFO

Polenta is a typical Italian dish made of finely ground cornmeal.

To prepare, bring 3¹/₄ cups (750 ml) salt water to a boil and trickle in 9 oz (250 g) cornmeal. Stir, ensuring the mixture is free of lumps.

Allow the polenta to thicken, stirring constantly, for about 20 minutes, until the mass is so thick that the spoon stands up. Smooth out on a floured surface.

Cut the desired shapes out of the polenta.

Either serve the polenta pieces immediately, or fry them in hot butter until crisp and golden brown. If fried in butter, polenta will also taste good the next day.

SAUCES
for pork medallions

These creamy sauces will go particularly well with pork medallions fried in oil or clarified butter. You can choose between hot and sweet, savory and alcoholic, and a spicy oriental version.

Bell pepper and chile sauce

Dice 1 yellow bell pepper and cut $^1/_2$ a pitted chile into thin rings. Sweat in the meat juices. Add ketchup and some bouillon. Season to taste with sugar, salt, and pepper.

Brandy and cream sauce

Add bouillon, white wine, and a little brandy to the meat juices. Reduce with light cream and season to taste with salt and pepper. A good accompaniment to medallions in garlic and rosemary marinade.

Onion and curry cream

Sweat some onion wedges in the meat juices, then dust with flour and curry powder. Add light cream and bouillon, heat, and season with salt and pepper.

... with apples, cranberries, and Gouda

Brown 8 thick apple rings in 3 tablespoons butter. Then brown the medallions for 3 minutes and place on a baking sheet. Cover with the apple rings, dot with cranberry sauce, and sprinkle with 7 oz (200 g) grated Gouda. Bake for 10 minutes at 400 °F/200 °C. Dice generous 1 lb (500 g) apples and 1 onion, brown, then add 2 tablespoons Calvados, $^1/_2$ cup (125 ml) light cream, and 7 tablespoons (100 ml) meat bouillon. Serve the medallions with the sauce.

... with garlic and rosemary marinade

Combine 4 tablespoons olive oil, 1 teaspoon salt, 1 crushed garlic clove, pepper, and rosemary to make a marinade. Marinade the meat for at least 2 hours, wrapped in aluminum foil in the icebox. Then fry in olive oil until golden brown. Rewrap in foil. Place in an ovenproof dish and bake at 350 °F/175 °C for about 15 minutes, depending on the thickness of the meat.

PORK MEDALLIONS
several variations

These pieces of meat are called "medallions" because they are round or slightly oval, but at the same time the term also hints at a noble origin—which is reasonable, after all, as the meat comes from the best cut of pork: the tenderloin.

... with apricots and Gorgonzola

Brown the medallions for 3 minutes. Slice 1 garlic clove and sauté with the meat for 2 minutes. Drain 12 canned apricot halves and cut $5^1/_2$ oz (150 g) Gorgonzola into slices about $^1/_8$ in. (3 mm) thick. Season the medallions with salt and pepper and place in an ovenproof dish. Top each medallion with an apricot half and a slice of Gorgonzola. Bake for about 10 minutes at 400 °F/200 °C.

... with leeks and plums

Season the medallions with salt and pepper, and wrap them in leek leaves, halved lengthways. Fasten with toothpicks. Fry in 5 tablespoons butter for 5–7 minutes each side, depending on thickness. Remove from the pan and keep warm. Add 3 tablespoons brandy and 7 oz (200 g) pitted plums to the pan, heat gently, and serve with the medallions.

... with herb butter breadcrumbs

Knead $5^1/_2$ oz (150 g) butter with 1 bunch chopped thyme and 1 cup (100 g) dried breadcrumbs. Fry the medallions for 2 minutes each side, then place in an ovenproof dish. Cover with the breadcrumb mixture. Bake at 350 °F/175 °C for about 10 minutes.

... with scallions and mustard

Cut 1 onion and 4 oz (120 g) scallions into strips. Fry the onion in 1 tablespoon oil and the scallions in 1 tablespoon each butter and oil, then combine. Allow to cool, then mix with 1 oz (25 g) grated Gouda, 1 tablespoon mustard, dried breadcrumbs, salt, and pepper. Brown the medallions, place them in an ovenproof dish, and cover with the onion mixture. Bake at 400 °F/200 °C for about 10 minutes.

RIB AND SHORT LOIN STEAKS
with onions

Serves 4

4	*short loin steaks, each about 7 oz (200 g)*
	Pepper
	Flour
7 tbsp (100 ml)	*oil*
	Salt
²/₃ cup (150 ml)	*meat bouillon*
4	*onions, finely sliced in rings*

INFO

With onion steaks, **onions**—the name's a giveaway—play a large part. The list of uses for onions in the kitchen is almost endless, and they form the foundation of many tasty meals. This versatility has also given rise to the huge range of onion varieties: large and small, and from mild through sweet to bitingly hot. In gourmet cooking, terms such as "à la soubise" or "à la lyonnaise" always indicate a generous use of onions.

Step by step

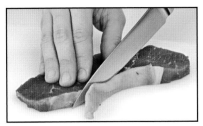

Trim any fat and sinew off the steaks. Pat dry and press flat.

Sprinkle both sides of the steaks with freshly ground pepper, and turn them in flour.

Heat half the oil in a pan. Fry the steaks over medium heat, for about 4 minutes each side.

Remove the steaks from the pan, season, cover, and keep warm. Add the bouillon to the pan juices and reduce.

Fry the onions in the remaining oil until golden brown.

Put the steaks on the plates, pour over the sauce, and cover with the onions.

Side dish

The best side dish for short loin steaks with onions is **pan-fried potatoes**. To make, boil 1³/₄ lb (800 g) unpeeled potatoes in a large pan of salt water. Once cooked and cooled, peel and quarter the potatoes. Heat 5 tablespoons oil in a skillet and fry the potatoes over high heat, turning several times, until crisp and golden brown. Finally, season with freshly ground salt and pepper, sprinkle with finely chopped parsley, and serve immediately.

SIDE DISHES
for rib and short loin steaks

Pasta or rice go well with these steaks—as do various potato dishes. Here are two suggestions:

RIB AND SHORT
several

Both rib and short loin steaks can be used for these dishes. The rib and short loin are two adjacent beef cuts from the back of the animal, the short loin being further back, behind the rib cut in the front. Finger-thick steaks are prepared from these cuts and

Potato au gratin
Slice the potatoes very thinly and layer them in a baking pan, slightly overlapping. Season with salt, pepper, and nutmeg. Cover with a mixture of light cream, milk, and grated Gouda, and bake for 50–60 minutes at 400 °F/200 °C.

... with bell peppers and green peppercorns
Season the steaks and brown them. Remove from the pan. Slice 2 bell peppers (one red, one green) into fine strips and sweat with 1 sliced Spanish onion. Make a sauce by adding 7 tablespoons (100 ml) of bouillon and 2 tablespoons ice-cold butter to the meat pan juices. Add 1 tablespoon pickled green peppercorns. Serve the steaks together with the vegetables and sauce.

Potato purée
Boil the potatoes in their skins, peel, and put through a ricer while still hot. Gradually stir in milk and butter until a creamy consistency is achieved. Season with salt and nutmeg.

... with mustard, cranberries, and sour cream
Season the steaks with salt and pepper, and spread one side thickly with mustard. Fry on the mustard side first, then on the other, and remove from the pan. Sweat 1 finely chopped onion in the pan until transparent, then add some water. Pour into a saucepan and bind the sauce with flour. Add the meat and 2 tablespoons cranberry sauce, and cook until done. Before serving, stir in $^1/_2$ cup (125 ml) sour cream.

LOIN STEAKS
v a r i a t i o n s

can be served quick-fried. These steaks are particularly suitable for highly flavored dishes. The ideal complements for these robust steaks are garlic, onions, leek, herbs, and mustard. Here, we bring you four suggestions for different recipes.

SALADS
for rib and short loin steaks

Salads also go very well with these steaks—traditional or made of various kinds of raw vegetables and fruit. Here are two suggestions:

... with garlic and parsley sauce

Season and brown the steaks. Remove from the pan. Thinly slice 3 garlic cloves, sauté in the pan, and set aside. Make a sauce by adding 7 tablespoons (100 ml) bouillon and 2 tablespoons ice-cold butter, $1/2$ bunch finely chopped parsley, and 1 teaspoon sweet paprika to the pan juices. Serve the meat with the sauce, with the sautéed garlic scattered over the top.

Red cabbage and apple salad

Grate the red cabbage and combine with a grated, fairly acid apple and some lemon juice. Stir in a dressing of wine vinegar, salt, white pepper, and light cream.

... with a soy sauce and leek marinade, and sesame

Mix 1 thinly sliced leek, 1 finely diced onion, 4 crushed garlic cloves, 2 tablespoons sugar, 2 tablespoons sesame oil, 4 tablespoons soy sauce, and 4 tablespoons white wine to make a marinade. Add the steaks and mix well. Allow to stand for 1–2 hours in the icebox. Then fry in the pan in 2 tablespoons of sesame oil. Serve sprinkled with 3 tablespoons sesame seeds.

Mâche (corn salad)

Remove the roots from the mâche, wash the leaves, and dry well in a salad spinner. Toss in a dressing of vinegar, oil, salt, pepper, and sugar. Sprinkle croutons on top.

MEAT SKEWERS

with bacon, onions, and tomatoes

Serves 4

4 tbsp	oil
	Pepper
	Salt
1 tsp generous	rosemary
1 lb (500 g)	beef, pork, or lamb, cut 1½ in. (3–4 cm) x 1½ in. (1 cm) thick
5½ oz (150 g)	bacon, cut 1½ in. (3–4 cm) x ½ in. (1 cm) thick
2	onions, cut into thick wedges
2	tomatoes, cut into quarters
1 tbsp	oil
4	skewers (wood or metal)

Step by step

Prepare a marinade from the oil, pepper, salt, and rosemary.

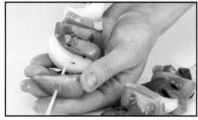

Brush the skewers carefully with oil and allow to drain.

Add the meat to the marinade, cover, and leave in the icebox for at least 10 hours. Turn the meat from time to time.

Also brush the grill or barbecue rack with oil. Place the skewers under the grill, 2 in. (5 cm) apart.

Push the meat onto the skewers, alternating with the bacon, onion, and tomato pieces.

Grill for 10–15 minutes, turning several times. Serve immediately.

BARBECUING INFO

There are now many different kinds of equipment available for **barbecuing**. You can choose between the classic charcoal barbecue, gas, lava rock, or electric grills—depending on your needs and preferences. Typical herbs for barbecues are:

Thyme,

Rosemary,

Oregano,

Sage.
And, of course, any others you might like.

If you use **wooden skewers**, remember to soak them well in water beforehand. This should stop them catching fire while you grill. It can happen very quickly when barbecuing, as the coals become very hot and it isn't always possible to prevent flames shooting up.

49

MEAT SKEWERS
several variations

There are no limits to your imagination when it comes to meat skewers: anything you can stick on a skewer and fry, bake, or grill is possible—whatever tastes good is allowed. The marinade keeps the meat juicy and gives it more flavor.

... with shrimp, bell peppers, and Cape gooseberries

Season the meat with salt and pepper. Cut 2 onions and 4 red bell peppers into pieces. Wrap 12 shrimp individually in a half rasher of bacon or half slice of fresh ham. Push the pieces onto skewers, alternating shrimp, meat, onions, and bell peppers. Leave to stand for 6 hours in a marinade of 10 blanched and puréed Cape gooseberries, 3 tablespoons olive oil, 4 tablespoons balsamic vinegar, the juice of 1 lime, 1 tablespoon lime cordial, 2 tablespoons paprika paste, salt, and pepper.

... with ginger and peanut butter

Cut the meat into 4 strips and fold each one onto a skewer, to form a wavy shape. Brush with a marinade of finely chopped ginger and 8 tablespoons teriyaki sauce. Sauté 1 diced onion, mix with $5^1/_2$ oz (150 g) unsweetened peanut butter, 1 teaspoon sambal ulek chile paste, 4 tablespoons soy sauce, and 7 tablespoons (100 ml) pineapple juice. Baste the skewers with the marinade when grilling.

... with liver, green bell pepper, and gherkins

Dice 3 green bell peppers, 7 oz (200 g) each of pig's liver and bacon, and place on skewers with 3 slices of gherkin per skewer and 3 onions cut into wedges. Prepare a sauce of 3 oz (80 g) ketchup, 2 tablespoons curry powder, 1 tablespoon apricot jelly, salt, and pepper. Pour half over the meat skewers and bake for 1 hour at 350 °F/180 °C. Turn the skewers from time to time, and baste with the rest of the sauce.

... with garlic, zucchini, and cherry tomatoes

Mix 3 crushed garlic cloves with 7 tablespoons (100 ml) olive oil, 1 tablespoon lemon juice, 2 tablespoons mustard, 1 tablespoon thyme, salt, and pepper. Marinate the meat in the mixture for about 2 hours. Cut the zucchini into pieces about 1 in. (2.4 cm) long. Halve 4–6 garlic cloves (according to taste). Place alternate pieces of meat, zucchini, garlic, and a total of 12 cherry tomatoes on the skewers, and grill.

SAUCES
for meat skewers

For sauce fans, we've added 3 delicious sauces to the 6 different meat skewer recipes. These sauces will also go well with other quick-fried or grilled meats.

Curry and pineapple sauce
Mix canned pineapple cubes with 1 thinly sliced, pitted chile. Mix 7 tablespoons (100 ml) pineapple juice with the same amount of water, 1 pinch bouillon granules, and curry powder to taste, to make a creamy sauce. Stir in the pineapple and chile.

Onion sauce
Chop pickled pearl onions and mix with white wine and crème fraîche. Season with salt, pepper, and chopped rosemary. Goes well with apricot and pearl onion skewers.

Bell pepper and mushroom sauce
Sauté thinly sliced mushrooms with strips of red and yellow bell pepper and a chopped onion. Stir in some light cream and season. Goes well with the liver and green bell pepper skewers.

... with apricots and pearl onions
Brown 9 oz (250 g) onion rings. Add 4^1/$_2$ oz (125 g) apricot jelly mixed with 2 tablespoons vinegar, 1 teaspoon sugar, 1 crushed garlic clove, salt, and pepper, and simmer for 5 minutes. Alternate the meat, 4^1/$_2$ oz (125 g) bacon rashers, and 9 oz (250 g) dried apricots, soaked, on skewers, leave to marinate overnight, and grill.

... with pineapple, boiled ham, and Gouda
Season the meat with salt, pepper, 2 teaspoons paprika, and 1 tablespoon curry powder. Stir 2 crushed garlic cloves into 2 tablespoons oil and brush the meat with the mixture. Cut 5^1/$_2$ oz (150 g) boiled ham slices in half, roll them up, and alternate on skewers with 7 oz (200 g) canned pineapple pieces and the meat. Brown under the grill, sprinkle with 5^1/$_2$ oz (150 g) grated Gouda, and bake for 10 minutes in the oven.

GROUND MEAT

Ground meat is so wonderfully versatile!

You can make it into patties or meatloaf, add tasty ingredients to the meat mixture, wrap it in pastry, and conjure up delicious sauces for baked or pan dishes.

Everything is possible—and very easy!

In this chapter, you'll find not only as many recipes and variations as you could want, but also side dishes and sauces to accompany them.

MEATBALLS

Königsberger Klöpse (traditional German meatball dish)

Serves 4

1 lb (500 g)	mixed ground meat (beef and pork)
2	onions, one diced
1 bunch	parsley, finely chopped
4	anchovies, finely chopped
1 tbsp	light cream
	Salt, pepper, ground nutmeg, marjoram
1	egg
1	stale bread roll, soaked
1	bay leaf
2	cloves
3 tbsp	butter
3 tbsp	flour
2 tbsp	lemon juice
2 tbsp	capers
3 tbsp	sour cream

Step by step

Mix together the ground meat, diced onion, parsley, anchovies, cream, spices, egg, and bread roll, squeezed out.

For the sauce, melt the butter, add the flour, and cook until golden brown. Gradually stir in 2 cups (500 ml) of the cooking liquid.

Bring 4 cups (1 liter) salt water to a boil, reduce the heat to medium, and add the bay leaf and whole onion studded with the cloves.

Cook the sauce for 20 minutes then add the lemon juice, capers, and sour cream. Season with salt, pepper, and nutmeg.

Shape the ground meat mixture into balls 2–2 1/2 in. (5–6 cm) across, steep in the hot water for 15–20 minutes, set aside, and retain the liquid.

Spoon the meatballs into the sauce.

MEATBALLS
several variations

Meatballs in lots of sauce are not just a favorite meal for children. Serve them with rice, pasta, potatoes, corn... or just bread. A hearty meal to satisfy everyone!

... with tomato sauce and mozzarella

Briefly sweat 1 diced onion in 2 tablespoons tomato paste. Add 9 oz (250 g) sieved tomatoes and 2 crushed garlic cloves, and season with salt, pepper, Italian herbs, and sugar. Simmer for 30 minutes. Combine generous 1 lb (500 g) ground meat with $^2/_3$ cup (100 g) all-purpose flour, 1 egg, chile powder, salt, pepper, and herbs, and shape into meatballs. Pour over the sauce, top with $4^1/_2$ oz (125 g) grated mozzarella, and bake for 10–15 minutes.

... with potatoes and zucchini

Chop an onion and a garlic clove then mix with 1 tablespoon mustard and generous 1 lb (500 g) ground meat. Season with salt and pepper. Shape the meatballs, fry for about 5 minutes, and remove from the pan. Fry $1^3/_4$ lb (750 g) diced potatoes and 2 sliced zucchini in the pan, add a little water, 7 tablespoons (100 ml) light cream, and generous $^3/_4$ cup (200 ml) milk, simmer for 10 minutes, bind the sauce, and bring to a boil. Add the meatballs and season with salt and pepper.

... with quark, cucumber, and mint

Knead together 1 finely diced onion, 1 stale bread roll (previously soaked), generous 1 lb (500 g) ground meat, 1 egg, salt, and cayenne. Shape into meatballs and fry for 10 minutes. Stir 1 grated cucumber, $^1/_2$ bunch chopped mint, and 4 crushed garlic cloves into generous 1 lb (500 g) low-fat quark and $^2/_3$ cup (150 ml) sour cream. Adjust the seasoning and add the meatballs.

... with carrots, onions, and curry powder

Mix together generous 1 lb (500 g) ground meat, dried breadcrumbs, 1 egg, salt, and pepper and shape into meatballs. Fry for about 10 minutes then remove from the pan. Peel and slice generous 1 lb (500 g) carrots and sweat in oil with 1 diced onion. Add 2 tablespoons each curry powder and all-purpose flour, and cook lightly. Stir in 2 cups (500 ml) bouillon and simmer for 10 minutes. Add 1 cup (250 ml) crème fraîche, $^1/_2$ bunch chopped parsley, and finally the meatballs.

... with peanuts, coconut milk, and bell peppers

Mix together 1³/₄ oz (50 g) finely chopped peanuts, 1 crushed garlic clove, 3 tablespoons fish sauce, 2 teaspoons curry paste, salt, pepper, and generous 1 lb (500 g) ground beef. Shape into meatballs and roll them in 4 tablespoons cornstarch. Fry the meatballs, remove from the pan, and set aside. Chop 2 bunches of scallions into rings, slice 2 red bell peppers into strips, and sweat them in the pan juices. Stir in 3¹/₃ cups (800 ml) coconut milk and 1 teaspoon sugar, add the meatballs, and bring to a boil.

... with mushrooms, bolete, and chanterelles

Combine generous 1 lb (500 g) ground meat, 1 chopped onion, 2 tablespoons quark, 1 tablespoon tomato paste, salt, pepper, and paprika. Shape into meatballs, fry for 10 minutes, and set aside. Sauté 1 diced onion in the pan. Add 5¹/₂ oz (150 g) soaked bolete, generous 1 lb (500 g) mushrooms, and 9 oz (250 g) chanterelles. Season, add bouillon, simmer for 5 minutes, and bind the sauce. Add the meatballs and simmer briefly.

SIDE DISHES
for meatballs

Potatoes, boiled or baked, go well with both mild and spicy recipes.

Duchess potatoes

Stir 7 tablespoons (100 g) butter, 4 egg yolks, salt, pepper, and nutmeg into 1³/₄ lb (800 g) creamed potatoes. Pipe the potato into small piles on a greased baking sheet. Brush with beaten egg yolk and bake for 10 minutes at 425 °F/220 °C.

Dauphine potatoes

Bring ³/₄ cup (200 ml) water to a boil with 2¹/₂ tablespoons (40 g) butter and a little salt, then remove from the heat. Add 5 tablespoons all-purpose flour and return to the heat, stirring until a lump of dough is formed and sticks to the bottom. Gently beat in 4 eggs, season with salt, and add creamed potatoes. Shape into dumplings with a spoon and fry in hot oil until golden brown.

Boiled potatoes

Peel and halve 1³/₄ lb (800 g) potatoes. Boil in a pan of salt water until done. Turn off the heat and leave the potatoes uncovered in the pan to allow the steam to dissipate.

GOUND MEAT PATTIES
with onions, gherkins, and mustard

INFO

The classic flavoring for **pickles** is a blend of vinegar and herbs in which gherkins are pickled. The pickling liquid often contains dill, white mustard seeds, onions, and possibly even sugar, plus flavoring such as pepper. For mustard pickles, on the other hand, medium-size cucumbers are used, also pickled in a special vinegar and mustard seed liquid. Gherkins pickled in brine are preserved by lactic acid fermentation.

Serves 4

1	*stale bread roll*
1 large	*onion, finely chopped*
5	*gherkins, finely chopped*
9 oz (250 g)	*ground beef*
9 oz (250 g)	*ground pork*
1	*egg*
2 tbsp (30 ml)	*red wine*
2 tsp	*mustard*
	Salt
	Pepper
2 tbsp	*butter*

Step by step

Soak the bread roll in 1 cup (250 ml) water, then squeeze it out thoroughly and crumble with your hands.

Mix the onion and gherkins with the ground meat, bread roll, egg, red wine, mustard, salt, and pepper.

With moistened hands, shape 8 flattened, roughly tennis-ball size patties.

Heat the butter in a skillet over medium heat. Slide the patties in one after another, using a spatula.

Fry for 4 minutes, then turn and fry over reduced heat for 5 minutes each side, until crispy and brown.

Side dish

Just about any cooked vegetables will go with patties. The combination of **peas and carrots** is very popular and, for many of us, will awaken childhood memories: sweat 4 large carrots and 3^1/$_2$ oz (100 g) frozen peas in 1 teaspoon butter, season with salt, and add a little sugar. Pour in some water and simmer for 5–10 minutes in a covered pan. Season to taste with salt and pepper, and stir in 1 tablespoon chopped parsley.

Side dish

Sometimes the simplest solution is the best. Serve **potatoes boiled in their skins** with your patties. Cooking is less work, and teamwork peeling the potatoes at the table can be fun. This is how you do it: thoroughly scrub 1^3/$_4$ lb (750 g) non-floury potatoes with a vegetable brush, under running water. Boil for about 20 minutes in plenty of salt water, drain, and serve. Don't forget to provide a knife for each guest to peel their potatoes.

GROUND MEAT

SAUCES
for patties

Dark, flavorsome sauces are an excellent complement to the hearty taste of patties! The basic sauce can be deliciously flavored with various ingredients such as mustard, green pepper, paprika, tomato paste, brandy, cream, or crème fraîche.

... with mushrooms and parsley

Sweat 1 finely chopped onion until soft, add 1 crushed garlic clove and $3^1/_2$ oz (100 g) thinly sliced mushrooms, and cook until almost all the liquid has evaporated. Leave to cool then mix with ground meat and 1 finely chopped bunch parsley. Season with salt, pepper, thyme, and paprika, shape the patties, and fry.

Dark mustard sauce

Make a sauce from meat bouillon cooked with a carrot, an onion, and a stick of celery. Add red wine and herbs to taste, and bind the sauce with butter or a flour roux. Then flavor the sauce with 1–2 tablespoons mustard and add some green peppercorns. This makes a good accompaniment to hearty patty recipes with mustard, paprika, onions, tomatoes, and garlic.

... with whole grain mustard and paprika

Crumble 1 stale bread roll and soak in a little lukewarm milk. Add an egg, a little salt, pepper, and paprika, 2–3 teaspoons whole grain mustard, 2 finely chopped onions, and generous 1 lb (500 g) ground meat. Mix well. Shape into meatballs while heating 3 tablespoons butter in a skillet. Fry until brown on both sides and drizzle with the meat juices.

Hungarian sauce

Make the sauce described above and season until spicy with hot or sweet paprika and tomato paste. If you like it even hotter, add $1^1/_2$ teaspoon cayenne or a few drops of Tabasco® Sauce. Goes well with the hearty patty recipes described above.

PATTIES
several variations

Call it a patty, serve it in a bun and call it a hamburger, use beef, or pork, or lamb—these flattened, fried meatballs have many different names and even more different options for serving.

... with bananas, chile, and herbs

Finely chop 1 onion, 2 garlic cloves, 1 chile, and 1 handful fresh herbs (thyme, oregano, cilantro, and basil). Mix with 1 cup (100 g) dried breadcrumbs, a mashed banana, and the ground meat. Allow to stand for about 30 minutes, then season to taste with pepper, salt, ground coriander seeds, paprika, and a little lemon juice. Shape into patties and fry in olive oil.

... with pineapple and Gouda

Mix together 1 finely chopped onion and 1 soaked, well squeezed, stale bread roll, ground meat, 1 egg, a little chopped mint, salt, and pepper. Shape into 8 patties and brown them in 2 tablespoons butter. Fry 8 pineapple slices in 2 tablespoons butter and place one on each patty. Top each with a slice of Gouda and bake in the oven for 3 minutes at 425 °F/220 °C.

... with tomatoes and mozzarella

Finely dice 1 onion and 3 sun-dried tomatoes. Mix with ground meat, 1 egg, 1 soaked bread roll, 1 teaspoon pizza seasoning, salt, and pepper. Shape into 8 patties. Fry for 4 minutes each side then place on a baking sheet. Top each patty with 1 slice of tomato and 1 slice mozzarella. Bake for 8–10 minutes at 400 °F/200 °C.

... with Feta, Parmesan, and garlic

Thoroughly knead together the ground beef, 2 finely chopped garlic cloves, 7 oz (200 g) grated Parmesan, 5 1/2 oz (150 g) crumbled Feta, 1 finely diced tomato, 1 egg, 4 teaspoons bouillon, salt, and pepper. Mix 1 3/4 oz (50 g) Parmesan with 3 tablespoons all-purpose flour, coat the patties in the mixture, and fry until brown.

GROUND MEAT INFO

Ground meat is minced beef, pork, or lamb with the coarse sinews removed. There is a difference between ground meat and the ground steak used for beef tartare, because the latter

must not contain any fat and be beef only. German "Mett" is ground meat or tartare prepared with salt and onions, and with other ingredients or spices added.

OVEN ROAST POTATOES INFO

For a classic meatloaf, you need side dishes that can handle its hearty flavor—such as potatoes.

Why not make use of the heat of the oven and prepare **oven roast potatoes** at the same time? To make, scrub the potatoes under running water, cut in half, place cut side down on a baking sheet, and brush with corn oil. Sprinkle with a little salt and add further seasoning if desired—for instance, paprika or rosemary.
Put the baking sheet in the oven with the meatloaf, and bake for about 45 minutes.

Serves 4

1	*stale bread roll*
2	*onions, finely chopped*
1	*crushed garlic clove*
14 oz (400 g)	*ground beef*
14 oz (400 g)	*ground pork*
1³/₄ oz (50 g)	*sausage meat (veal if available)*
2	*eggs*
	Salt
	Pepper
1 tsp	*thyme*
1 tsp	*rosemary*
3 tbsp	*oil for frying*
2 cups (500 ml)	*bouillon*
1	*carrot, chopped*

Step by step

Soak the bread roll, then squeeze out. Mix with 1 chopped onion and the garlic, ground meat, sausage meat, eggs, seasoning, and herbs.

Pour the bouillon into a roasting pan then add the carrots and remaining onion.

With moistened hands, shape the mixture into a round, slightly flattened meatloaf.

Add the meatloaf and bake at 350 °F/180 °C for about 45–60 minutes, until done.

Brown in oil in a skillet, for about 1 minute each side.

During cooking, turn the meatloaf and baste with the juices several times.

MEATLOAF
with garlic, thyme, and rosemary

SAUCES
for meatloaf

For a plain meatloaf, these classic sauces—cream, onion, or tomato—are an excellent accompaniment. Plus, they will make many of these suggested variations taste simply delicious.

Spicy tomato and mushroom sauce

Cut fresh mushrooms (common store mushrooms, oyster mushrooms, etc.) into small pieces. Sauté in olive oil and pour in some vegetable bouillon. Add chervil and dill, season with salt and pepper, and bind. Goes well with the ewe's milk cheese and "falscher Hase" recipes for meatloaf.

Hearty onion sauce

Sauté sliced onions, diced celery, and tomatoes cut into wedges in olive oil. Add meat bouillon, reduce, season with thyme, salt, pepper, and nutmeg, and bind. Goes well with the rosemary and thyme, ewe's milk cheese, and "falscher Hase" recipes for meatloaf.

Almond and tomato sauce

Briefly fry a whole clove of garlic in butter, add milk and ground almonds, and bring to a boil. Add the meatloaf juices and some tomato paste to the milk and almond mix, simmer, and season to taste with herbs. Goes well with all the meatloaf variations noted above.

MEATLOAF
several

Here's what makes meatloaf so popular—it tastes almost like roast meat, but is easier and quicker to prepare. It is also more economical, which makes it ideal for everyday meals. You can make a meatloaf with a mixture of ground pork and beef, or with beef or pork alone. The loaf is shaped from the ground meat mixture, which

... with ewe's milk cheese, bell pepper, and nuts

Dice 7 oz (200 g) ewe's milk cheese and 1 small red bell pepper. Fold the bell pepper, 3 tablespoons coarsely chopped filberts, and $2/3$ of the ewe's milk cheese into the ground meat mixture. Shape into a loaf and fry on all sides, then bake for 45 minutes at 350 °F/180 °C. Crumble the remaining ewe's milk cheese over the meatloaf and bake for a further 15 minutes.

... with bananas, almonds, and pepper

Flatten the meatloaf mixture. Season well with pepper, and wrap it around 1 peeled banana sprinkled with 2 tablespoons slivered almonds. Shape into a loaf. Fry on all sides then transfer to a roasting pan. Bake in the oven for about 1 hour, at 350 °F/180 °C.

SIDE DISHES
for meatloaf

can be treated like dough—flavorings and other ingredients are easily incorporated, with some being added chopped or even whole, such as the hard-boiled eggs in "falscher Hase."

These 3 sauce suggestions are also good for rounding off classic meatloaf—decide on your own particular favorite. Or, as we suggest here, try with all the variations.

Broccoli with cheese sauce

Cook 1$\frac{1}{4}$ lb (600 g) broccoli florets until al dente and season with salt. Heat a scant 7 tablespoons (100 ml) light cream with the same quantity of bouillon, reduce a little, and fold in 1$\frac{3}{4}$ oz (50 g) grated cheese. Season to taste with salt and pepper. Pour over the broccoli.

... with Roquefort and pears

Finely crumble 9 oz (250 g) Roquefort and add to the meatloaf mixture. Season with salt. Shape into a loaf and brown on all sides. Place in a roasting pan and add 3 canned pears, cut into halves, plus 1 cup (250 ml) dry white wine. Bake for about 1 hour at 350 °F/180 °C.

Buttered mixed vegetables

Thaw 7 oz (200 g) each frozen peas and carrots and cook in 4 tablespoons butter for about 3–4 minutes. Season to taste with salt and pepper. Add a few leaves of butter to serve.

... with eggs, mustard, and parsley ("falscher Hase")

"Falscher Hase" (literally, "false hare") is a traditional German meatloaf recipe. To make, put half the meatloaf mixture in a baking pan. Place 4 hard-boiled eggs in the middle, brush with a little mustard, and scatter with 3 tablespoons finely chopped parsley. Place the rest of the mixture on top and dot with butter. Bake for 45 minutes at 350 °F/180 °C, covered, then for a further 15 minutes uncovered.

Braised beets

Finely dice 14 oz (400 g) cooked beets. Sweat 1 peeled and chopped onion in a pan with 2 tablespoons butter until transparent. Add the beets and stir briefly. Season with salt and pepper.

HAMBURGERS
with onions, tomato, and gherkins

INFO

French fries are not just French—they're international. In France, they love their straw-thin "pommes pilles," matchstick "allumettes," boxy "Pont Neufs," and waffled "gauffrette" slices, while the Spanish cook their fries in olive oil. In the USA you can enjoy, among other variations, chunky Texas oven fries.
All in all, there's a huge selection from which to choose—thin, thick, straight, crinkle cut... (the wavy surface of the latter makes fries particularly crispy).

Serves 4

14 oz (400g)	ground meat
	Salt
	Pepper
3 tbsp	oil
4	burger buns
2 tsp	mayonnaise
4	lettuce leaves
3	tomatoes, thinly sliced
1	red onion, sliced into rings
2	gherkins, thinly sliced
1 tsp	mustard
1 tsp	ketchup

Step by step

Season the meat with salt and pepper and, with moistened hands, shape into 4 flat patties.

Fry in hot oil on both sides over high heat, until the burgers are crisp and brown.

Cut open the buns and lightly toast without fat, cut side only, in a skillet. Do not allow them to burn.

Spread mayonnaise on the bottom half of each bun and top with lettuce, tomato, onion, gherkin, and finally the burger.

Spread the top half of each bun with mustard and ketchup and place over the burgers.

Side dish

French fries are, of course, the classic hamburger side dish. If you want a lower fat option, don't deep-fry the potatoes, but instead try the following recipe: peel 6 potatoes and cut into sticks. Enclose in plastic wrap with 1 tablespoon oil and shake well, then spread on a baking sheet and roast for about 20 minutes at 350 °F/180 °C.

Salad

This tastes great with fries and hamburgers: **Salad with cocktail sauce dressing**. To make, simply mix together 1 teaspoon salt, 2 teaspoons sugar, 1 teaspoon mustard, 2 tablespoons tomato ketchup, 4 tablespoons evaporated milk, 2 tablespoons red wine vinegar, and 6 tablespoons corn oil. Mix carefully with shredded lettuce. If desired, add small pieces of tomato, cucumber, radish, or other salad vegetables of your choice.

GROUND MEAT

SAUCES
for hamburgers

You can see, just by looking at the recipe variations, that hamburgers can be prepared according to individual taste—but you will need a sauce. At least one of the three main flavoring ingredients—ketchup, mayonnaise, or mustard—simply has to be included. You can, of course, add more, so we've provided another sauce suggestion to extend your options. And if the meal has to be not just tasty, but healthy as well, you can always make your own ketchup.

Maple syrup and barbecue sauce
Fry a diced onion until transparent. Stir in barbecue sauce, maple syrup, wine vinegar, and brown sugar. Season to taste with Tabasco® Sauce and simmer for 2 minutes while stirring. Excellent with classic hamburgers, and hamburgers with caramelized onions.

Homemade ketchup
Simmer diced tomatoes and onions together with wine vinegar, sugar, salt, paprika, peppercorns, cloves, nutmeg, and Tabasco® Sauce for 20 minutes, then purée.
Bottle while still hot and leave to stand for 4 weeks.

... with cheese, mushrooms, and bacon
Fry 12 rashers bacon until crisp. Remove from the pan. Slice $3^1/_2$ oz (100 g) mushrooms and fry in the bacon fat. Then fry the burgers in the fat. Spread mayonnaise on the bun halves and layer a burger and 1 slice Gouda on each lower half. Broil until the cheese melts. Layer lettuce, sliced tomato, bacon, and mushrooms over the burger and cheese. Cover with the top half of the bun.

... with fried egg, pineapple, and beet
Combine the ground meat with 7 oz (200 g) diced bacon, 1 egg, salt, and pepper. Shape into burgers and fry; then fry 4 eggs in the same pan. Spread the bun halves with ketchup, mayonnaise, and mustard, then layer each burger in its bun with 1 slice Gouda, onion rings, sliced tomato, a lettuce leaf, 1 slice pickled beets, 1 pineapple ring, and 1 fried egg.

HAMBURGERS
several variations

Pre-formed meat officially sold as a "hamburger" may contain only ground beef and seasoning, with a maximum 30 percent fat by weight. Other ingredients are not permitted. Buy them or make them: the choice is yours!

... with poppy seed buns and Spanish onions

Lightly toast 4 poppy seed buns and spread both halves with ketchup. Place rings of Spanish onion on each bottom half, add a burger plus a leaf of iceberg lettuce, and cover with the top half of the bun.

... with milk bread buns, cucumber, and caramelized onions

Dice 2 onions and sauté in fat until crisp. Cut open 4 milk bread buns. Spread each of the lower halves with ketchup and mayonnaise. Layer with $1/2$ a sliced cucumber, then with the caramelized onions, and finally the burger. Add 1 lettuce leaf and cover with the top half of the roll.

... with mozzarella and scallions

Thinly slice 1 mozzarella ball, 4 gherkins, and 6 cherry tomatoes. Cut 3 scallions into rings. Halve the buns and spread inside with a mixture of ketchup, mayonnaise, and mustard. Layer with the ingredients and top with 1 shredded leaf of iceberg lettuce.

... with whiskey, Worcestershire sauce, and Cheddar

Mix together the ground meat, 1 finely diced onion, 1 crushed garlic clove, 1 teaspoon whiskey, and 1 tablespoon Worcestershire sauce. Season to taste with salt, pepper, paprika, and nutmeg. Fry 4 burgers and, just before the second side is done, top each one with 1 slice Cheddar. Allow to melt. Spread the halved buns with ketchup and mayonnaise, add the burgers, and layer.

BELL PEPPERS INFO

All kinds of **bell pepper** with a large enough space inside are suitable for filling. There are more than a thousand different varieties, although not all of

them, of course, are available for purchase. There are differences in shape, color, flavor, and hotness.

The fiery hot chile and slightly less biting pepperoncini are also members of the same family, the **capsicums**. The most commonly available bell peppers in green, red, orange, or yellow are very mild and excellent for filling. The green variety is simply a fruit that has been harvested when unripe; otherwise, it would be red.

Also available are the elongated **sweet peppers** in red, yellow, or white, and so-called white bell peppers.

Serves 4

³/₄ cup (150 g)	*rice*
8	*bell peppers (red, yellow, and green)*
1	*stale bread roll*
1³/₄ lb (500g)	*ground meat*
3	*crushed garlic cloves*
	Salt
	Pepper
	Marjoram
	Tomato sauce (see side dish recipe)

Step by step

Cook the rice and leave to cool. Cut the tops off the bell peppers. Remove the white pith and the seeds.

Stuff the hollows of the bell peppers with the mixture and cover with the tops.

Soak the bread roll in water until soft, press the liquid out thoroughly, and crumble.

Place in an ovenproof dish and pour over the tomato sauce.

Combine the ground meat, rice, bread roll, garlic, salt, pepper, and marjoram.

Bake in the oven for 40–50 minutes at 325 °F/160 °C.

GROUND MEAT FILLINGS
with rice for bell peppers

SAUCES
for ground meat

Use a savory sauce to turn pastry or vegetables filled with ground meat into a delicious, gourmet meal. Simply try out these sauces with the recipe variations.

Tomato sauce
Make a thick tomato sauce with canned tomatoes, vegetable bouillon, and 1 chopped onion sweated in butter until transparent. Season with salt and pepper.

Garlic and parsley sauce
Sweat some thinly sliced garlic in hot oil, but do not allow to color. Stir in chopped parsley. Suitable for all fillings.

Green herb sauce with Feta
Finely chop herbs such as chervil, parsley, and dill, mix with chicken bouillon and crème fraîche, and stir in some chopped Feta. Goes well with rice, mushroom, vegetable, and bacon fillings.

GROUND MEAT FILLINGS
several

Vegetable, pastry, and even meat can be stuffed with ground meat. Served with a delicious sauce, dishes like this are excellent if you want to surprise your guests! Choose pastry, vegetables, pancakes, or whatever you decide: though you'll find suggestions on this page, you can use any of these fillings for all

... with mushrooms for pasties
Combine 1¹/₃ cups (200 g) all-purpose flour, 6 tablespoons (90 g) butter, 2 eggs, and some salt. Keep cool. Brown 1 diced onion, the ground meat, and 7 oz (200 g) diced mushrooms, and season to taste with salt, pepper, thyme, and paprika. Cut 5-in. (12-cm) circles out of the pastry, divide the ground meat mixture between them, and fold over. Brush with egg yolk and bake at 400 °F/200 °C for 20 minutes.

... with bacon and onion, for stuffed cabbage leaves
Blanch 8 leaves white cabbage. Mix the ground meat with 1 egg, 1 soaked, stale bread roll, 1–2 tablespoons mustard, 1 diced onion, 2 tablespoons diced bacon, salt, pepper, and paprika. Divide among the cabbage leaves, roll up, and secure. Brown, pour on a little bouillon, and braise for about 30 minutes. Add generous ³/₄ cup (200 ml) light cream, reduce a little, and season with salt and pepper.

DIPS
for ground meat

of the above. Use the ground meat and mushroom filling for vegetables or the chopped meat and pine nuts in pastry. Or dream up some quite different combinations!

Serve a savory dip with herbs and spices to complement the fillings for pastry and vegetables and provide a refreshing touch.

... with mozzarella and herbs for strudel

Brown the meat. Chop 1 small zucchini, 1 carrot, 1 scallion, 1 red bell pepper, and 1 bunch fresh herbs. Cut 1 mozzarella ball into small pieces. Mix with the ground meat, 2 tablespoons ajvar, and 2 tablespoons crème fraîche. Spread the filling onto 1 pack ready-made filo pastry and roll into a strudel. Bake for about 20 minutes at 400 °F/200 °C.

Tsatsiki dip

Roughly grate a cucumber, sprinkle with salt, and leave to stand for 10 minutes. Drain thoroughly. Mix with yogurt and crushed garlic cloves and season to taste with salt and pepper. Goes well with rice, mushroom, and vegetable fillings.

Tomato and basil dip

Briefly sweat chopped onions and tomatoes, add bouillon or wine, reduce, season with salt and pepper, and gently stir in some basil. Goes well with rice, mushroom, and vegetable fillings.

... with pine nuts and golden raisins for zucchini

Brown 1 diced onion with the ground meat. Stir in 1³/₄ oz (50 g) pine nuts, 1³/₄ oz (50 g) golden raisins, salt, pepper, and 1 teaspoon cinnamon. Stuff generous 1 lb (500 g) small, halved, hollowed-out zucchini with the mixture, and brown in a little oil. Add 2 tablespoons tomato paste, some water, 1 crushed garlic clove, and 1 teaspoon dried mint, and simmer for 1 hour.

Chile and herb dip

Stir finely chopped shallots, garlic, and chile flakes or harissa into olive oil. Add freshly chopped rosemary. Suitable for all fillings.

GROUND MEAT BAKES

with fusilli, mushrooms, and broccoli

INFO

Originally, **endive** was grown only for its root and not the lettuce-like buds. The discovery of the culinary qualities of these buds, which need to be kept in the dark to remain white and low in bitter agents, is probably only due to chance. If the buds open out in the light and are stored, they turn green and soon become bitter. This is why they're always displayed for sale in covered boxes. Even so, you should discard the bitter parts of the stalk.

Serves 4

9 oz (250 g)	fusilli
generous 1 lb (500 g)	broccoli
1 tbsp	oil
generous 1 lb (500 g)	ground meat
4	onions, finely diced
9 oz (250 g)	mushrooms, thinly sliced
5 tbsp	tomato paste
7 oz (200 g)	tomatoes
	Salt
	Pepper
4$^{1}/_{2}$ oz (125 g)	mozzarella, diced

Step by step

Cook the pasta according to the packet instructions. Add the broccoli, cut into florets, and continue cooking for about 5 minutes. Drain in a colander.

Fry the ground meat, onions, and mushrooms for about 10 minutes then add the tomato paste and tomatoes. Bring to a boil and season with salt and pepper.

Layer the pasta and ground meat sauce in an ovenproof dish.

Scatter with diced mozzarella.

Bake in a pre-heated oven at 400 °F/200 °C for about 20–30 minutes, until crisp.

Side dish

A pasta bake like this is a meal in itself and doesn't really need a side dish. But a light, refreshing salad is a nice way to complement a bake. For example, you could try a refreshing **endive and apple salad**:

Cut 4 endive and 2 apples into bite-sized pieces. To make the dressing, stir together 4 tablespoons walnut oil, some salt, pepper, curry powder, and 4 tablespoons chopped walnuts. Combine with the salad.

Salad

A **frisée salad** is just as refreshing and easy to prepare. Cut a head of frisée into fine strips and soak briefly in warm water to draw out the bitter agents. Dry the salad thoroughly in a salad spinner.

Then, to make the dressing, mix 1 small diced onion with 3 tablespoons oil, 2 tablespoons vinegar, 1 pinch sugar, salt, and pepper. Fold into the salad.

GROUND MEAT BAKES
several variations

A hearty meal with cabbage, a hint of Asia with peaches and curry, or mild and savory with eggplant like the popular Greek moussaka... So many options, and the choice is yours.

... with rice and peaches

Brown the ground meat with 2 diced onions and season with salt and pepper. Mix with 7 oz (200 g) cooked rice. Alternate 14 oz (400 g) canned peach slices in an ovenproof dish with the ground beef mixture, finishing with a layer of peaches. Mix $^2/_3$ cup (150 ml) German curry ketchup with $^2/_3$ cup (150 ml) light cream and 7 tablespoons (100 ml) peach juice, bring to a boil, and pour over. Bake for 45 minutes at 350 °F/180 °C.

... with white cabbage, Gouda, and caraway

Sweat 2 finely chopped onions. Add the meat and brown it with the onions. Cook for 30 minutes with 14 oz (400 g) white cabbage cut into strips, 1 crushed garlic clove, paprika, 1 teaspoon caraway seeds, salt, and pepper. Transfer to an ovenproof dish and pour over 1 cup (250 ml) bouillon mixed with 3 tablespoons tomato paste, $3^1/_2$ oz (100 g) grated Gouda, and a mixture of 3 eggs, 1 cup (250 ml) milk, and salt. Bake for 45 minutes at 350 °F/180° C.

... with kale, potatoes, and bacon

Brown the ground meat with 2 diced onions. Add 3 tablespoons ketchup and 3 of crème fraîche. Blanch generous 1 lb (500 g) kale leaves and mix with $1^1/_4$ lb (600 g) diced potatoes. Layer in an ovenproof dish, starting with the vegetables then adding the ground meat mixture. Cover with 3 bacon rashers. Bake for 45 minutes at 350 °F/180 °C.

... with sweet potatoes and Emmental

Brown the ground meat with 1 diced onion and 1 crushed garlic clove, add 2 tablespoons tomato paste, and season with salt and pepper. In an ovenproof dish, alternate generous 1 lb (500 g) cooked and sliced sweet potatoes with the ground meat. Beat 2 eggs with generous $^3/_4$ cup (200 ml) light cream and pour over. Sprinkle with $3^1/_2$ oz (100 g) grated Emmental. Bake for 45 minutes at 350 °F/180 °C.

... with Schupfnudeln, sauerkraut, and Bergkäse

Sweat 9 oz (250 g) Schupfnudeln (German finger noodles—if not available, substitute gnocchi) in a little butter. Cook 11 oz (300 g) sauerkraut in a little vegetable bouillon and add 1 tablespoon tomato paste. Season the meat with salt and pepper and brown in some oil. In an ovenproof dish, mix the noodles/gnocchi with the sauerkraut and the meat mixture. Sprinkle with $3^1/_2$ oz (100 g) grated Bergkäse. Bake for 45 minutes at 350 °F/180 °C.

... with eggplant, tomato, and cinnamon (moussaka)

Mix the ground meat with garlic, salt, and pepper. Layer in an ovenproof dish with $1^3/_4$ lb (800 g) browned eggplant slices and 7 oz (200 g) sautéed diced onion. Top with a mixture of 9 oz (250 g) sliced tomatoes, 2 diced onions, and 1 crushed garlic clove, and pour over a reduced sauce of 2 egg yolks, $^1/_2$ cup (125 ml) milk, salt, pepper, and 1 teaspoon cinnamon. Bake for 45 minutes at 350 °F/180 °C.

SALADS
for bakes

These baked ground meat dishes are actually complete meals in themselves, but you can add a delicious salad with additional vitamins and minerals.

Feta salad with green bell pepper

Simply combine green bell peppers cut into strips, onion rings, diced Feta, and cucumber sliced very thinly into strips with a dressing of coarsely ground pepper, vinegar, and oil.

Bell pepper salad

Cut red and green bell peppers into very thin strips and slice some onions into rings. Make a dressing of lemon juice, salt, sugar, and oil and combine.

Beet salad

Prepare a dressing of vinegar, oil, sugar, salt, grated horseradish, finely chopped onion, and crushed caraway seeds. Mix with cooked and grated beets.

GROUND MEAT SAUCES—BOLOGNESE SAUCE
with bacon, carrots, and red wine

Serves 4

11 oz (300 g)	ground meat
1	onion, finely diced
1	carrot, finely diced
1	stalk celery, finely chopped
1³/₄ oz (50g)	bacon, finely diced
2 tbsp (30 g)	butter
³/₄ cup (200 ml)	dry red wine
³/₄ cup (200 ml)	meat bouillon
2	bay leaves
11 oz (300 g)	tomatoes
	Salt and pepper
	A little milk

Step by step

Mix the ground meat with the onion, carrot, celery, and diced bacon.

Pour boiling water over the tomatoes, peel, remove the stalk bed and seeds, and purée. Add to the sauce.

Fry the ground meat in the butter until it takes on a crumbly texture, then pour over the red wine and reduce.

Season with salt and pepper, and add a little milk.

Add half the bouillon and the bay leaves, allow to reduce, and gradually add the rest of the bouillon.

Allow to simmer for 1 hour (it takes this long for the sauce to become really creamy). If necessary, add more milk.

PASTA INFO

This classic bolognese sauce is served with **pasta**: for example, with home-made tagliatelle. It's also excellent with macaroni, fusilli, penne, and spaghetti—it's all a matter of taste.

Spaghetti is pasta made from durum wheat semolina. The strands are round in cross-section and, when cooked, measure about ¹/₂ in. (2 mm) in diameter and 12 in. (30 cm) in length. Very thin spaghetti is known as spaghettini and fat spaghetti as spaghettoni. Because it is so sinuous, spaghetti mixes well with sauces.

Fusilli is spiral pasta and especially good for sauces with larger pieces in them, as coarsely chopped ingredients cling more readily to this shape.

Tagliatelle is made by cutting strips about ³/₄ in. (18 mm) wide from rolled-out pasta dough (using a pasta machine or a knife).

GROUND MEAT

SAUCES
with ground meat

Sauces, sauces, sauces! If you didn't find what you wanted in the main recipe on page 79, or in the variations, here are 3 more suggestions for using ground meat in sauces:

"African-style" ground meat sauce

Season a ground meat sauce with apricot jelly, curry powder, vinegar, almonds, and golden raisins to taste. Add light cream and crème fraîche for smoothness.

Ground meat sauce with Gorgonzola

Add $3^1/_2$ oz (100 g) crumbled Gorgonzola to the browned meat, stir in some light cream, and season with salt and pepper.

Hot ground meat sauce

Add cayenne and Tabasco® Sauce to bolognese sauce. If it becomes too hot, add a little sour cream to make it milder.

... with sweet corn and peas

Sauté 1 diced onion and 2 crushed garlic cloves. Add the ground meat and fry until it takes on a crumbly texture. Season with salt and pepper. Continue cooking with 1 tablespoon each tomato paste and mustard. Add 7 tablespoons (100 ml) red wine and simmer for a few minutes. Add 2 cups (500 ml) bouillon and $2^1/_2$ oz (75 g) each canned sweet corn and peas. Bring to a boil and bind.

... with soy sauce, sour cream, and chives

Sauté 2 finely chopped onions, add the ground meat, and cook until brown and crumbly in texture, stirring continuously. Add 2 tablespoons soy sauce. Turn the heat down low and add 1 cup (250 ml) sour cream. Heat, stirring continuously, but do not allow to boil. Season to taste with salt and pepper. Scatter 1 bunch chopped chives over to finish.

GROUND MEAT SAUCES
several variations

The ground meat sauces below reflect the cuisine of many different countries: Far Eastern, Greek, Turkish... It's quite clear that, all over the world, people love ground meat. Here you'll find, not just six variations, but an extra three suggestions for sauces.

... with red lentils, tomatoes, and bell peppers

Sweat 1 finely chopped onion and 2 crushed garlic cloves until transparent. Add the ground meat and fry until it takes on a crumbly texture, stirring constantly. Add generous 1 lb (500 g) sieved tomatoes, 1 diced green bell pepper, and $5\frac{1}{2}$ oz (150 g) red lentils, cover, and cook for about 15 minutes. Season to taste with salt, pepper, paprika, and cayenne.

... with spinach and Parmesan

Blanch 11 oz (300 g) spinach, rinse in cold water, and drain. Sweat 2 finely chopped shallots and 1 crushed garlic clove until transparent, add the meat, and brown. Stir in generous 1 lb (500 g) canned tomatoes, the spinach, 1 tablespoon tomato paste, and 1 teaspoon oregano, and cook for 10 minutes. Season to taste with Tabasco® Sauce, pepper, salt, and sugar, and stir in 2 tablespoons grated Parmesan.

... with coriander, mint, and cumin

Sauté 1 finely chopped onion, add the ground meat, and cook until it is brown and crumbly in texture, stirring continuously. Add 2 tablespoons cumin, 1 teaspoon paprika, and $\frac{1}{2}$ teaspoon ground coriander. Stir vigorously. Heat 4 tablespoons tomato paste in a skillet and pour in 2 cups bouillon. Add 1 bay leaf, sugar, salt, pepper, cinnamon, and $\frac{1}{2}$ teaspoon curry powder. Strip the leaves from 3 mint sprigs, tear into small pieces, and stir in.

... with Feta and kidney beans

Fry the ground meat until it takes on a crumbly texture and season with salt and pepper. Add $3\frac{1}{2}$ oz (100 g) finely diced Feta and 1 tablespoon tomato paste and simmer for a few minutes. Then add generous 1 lb (500 g) sieved tomatoes and 1 can kidney beans. Simmer for a further 10 minutes. Finally, add 2–3 tablespoons light cream and season to taste.

PEPPERCORN INFO

Pepper is the most important spice in the world's kitchens—so essential is this ingredient that wars have been fought over it in the past. The most important culinary types of peppercorn are as follows:

White peppercorn is quite mild, as the black rind is removed during fermentation.

Green peppercorn is harvested while still unripe. It is usually preserved in vinegar or quick-dried in a special process so that it keeps its green color.

Red peppercorn consists of ripe, unpeeled berries and, like green peppercorn, is mostly preserved in brine or pickled.

Black peppercorn is the whole berry, harvested unripe then dried, including the flesh of the fruit, which gives this pepper its heat.

Szechuan pepper is made from the fruit of the pepper tree and is named for the Chinese province.

82

Serves 4

generous 1 lb (500 g)	*potatoes, peeled and diced*
3 tbsp	*oil*
	Salt
	Some bouillon
generous 1 lb (500 g)	*ground meat*
7 oz (200 g)	*boiled ham, cut into strips*
6	*gherkins, finely diced*
5$^1/_2$ oz (150 g)	*mustard*
generous $^3/_4$ cup (200 ml)	*crème fraîche*
	Pepper
$^1/_2$	*bunch chives, chopped*

Step by step

Fry the diced potatoes in the oil with a little salt, until slightly crispy.

Add the ham, potatoes and gherkins to the meat and continue cooking.

Pour in the bouillon, cover, and simmer for about 10 minutes.

Stir in the mustard and crème fraîche and cook until a crust forms on the bottom of the pan.

Heat the ground meat in a skillet without oil until the texture is crumbly and dry.

Serve with freshly ground pepper and chopped chives.

GROUND MEAT PAN FRY
with potatoes and boiled ham

GROUND MEAT PAN FRIES
several variations

Ground meat pan fries are ideal for a quick meal, as they really are ready in next to no time. Side dishes don't need a great deal of effort either—serve some fresh bread and you have the perfect meal.

... with green bell peppers and peas

Fry 2 finely chopped onions and 1 crushed garlic clove with the ground meat until crumbly. Add 3 tablespoons white wine and season with 1 tablespoon paprika, salt, pepper, marjoram and thyme. Add 3 tablespoons tomato paste, generous 1 lb (500 g) canned tomatoes, 3 thinly sliced carrots, 3 diced green bell peppers, and $3\frac{1}{2}$ oz (100 g) peas, and cook for 10–15 minutes.

... with eggplant, tomatoes, and mushrooms

Fry the ground meat in 5 tablespoons garlic butter with 2 finely diced onions and 2 chopped scallions until it has a crumbly texture. Add 5 diced potatoes, generous 1 lb (500 g) diced eggplant, and $3\frac{1}{2}$ oz (100 g) common store mushrooms. Cook for 10–15 minutes. Add 11 oz (300 g) diced tomatoes, 1 tablespoon tomato paste, salt, pepper, paprika, and marjoram, simmer for a further 10 minutes, and season to taste.

... with rice, peaches, and leeks

Fry the ground meat with 1 finely diced onion until crumbly and season with salt and lemon pepper. Add 1 sliced leek and sauté with the meat and onion. Then add 1 cup (250 ml) bouillon and 9 oz (250g) canned peach slices, and cook over low heat. Mix $\frac{3}{4}$ cup (200 ml) crème fraîche with 2-3 tablespoons peach juice. Stir 7 oz (200 g) cooked rice into the meat mixture and finally add the crème fraîche.

... with zucchini, red bell peppers, and chorizo

Fry the ground meat until it takes on a crumbly texture then season with salt and pepper. Add 11 oz (300 g) each coarsely diced zucchini, diced red bell peppers, and diced potatoes, plus 1 diced onion, 1 crushed garlic clove, and $5\frac{1}{2}$ oz (150 g) chorizo. Pour in 1 cup (250 ml) bouillon, add 1 teaspoon mixed herbs, and cook over medium heat for about 15 minutes. Season to taste with salt, pepper, and 4 tablespoons light cream.

... with broccoli, green beans, and lentils

Blanch 3¹/₂ oz (100 g) each broccoli florets and green beans. Sweat in 1 tablespoon oil with 1 red bell pepper, cut into strips. Add 3¹/₂ oz (100 g) chopped mushrooms. Season with salt and pepper. Remove the vegetables and fry the ground meat in the pan. Return the vegetables to the pan with 3¹/₂ oz (100 g) cooked brown lentils.

... with white cabbage, celeriac, and fusilli

Sweat 9 oz (250 g) white cabbage, cut into strips, for about 5 minutes in 2 tablespoons oil, then do the same with 3¹/₂ oz (100 g) celeriac. Season with salt and pepper, remove from the pan, add the ground meat, and brown. Season with salt. Cook 9 oz (250 g) fusilli until al dente then mix with the vegetables and meat. Season to taste with Chinese five-spice powder and 4 tablespoons soy sauce.

DIPS
for pan fries

A refreshing yogurt and quark dip tastes especially delicious. You can find two variations below, one with cheese and one with vegetables. Of course, you can also choose other ingredients to suit your taste: for instance, garlic, celery, or horseradish.

Yogurt and quark dip with Gorgonzola

Stir yogurt, quark, and sour cream together and season with salt and pepper. Mix with 3¹/₂ oz (100 g) finely crumbled Gorgonzola, 2 tablespoons chopped chives, and 1 teaspoon paprika. This is excellent for the pan fries with potatoes and gherkins, bell peppers and peas, rice and peaches, and white cabbage and celeriac. To make the yogurt dip especially creamy, make it with crème fraîche.

Yogurt and quark dip with cucumber and tomatoes

Stir together yogurt, quark, and sour cream, plus salt and pepper. Add ¹/₄ peeled and finely diced cucumber and 1 diced tomato. Excellent for the pan fries with bell pepper and peas, eggplant and tomato, fennel and bacon, and zucchini and chorizo. Instead of the fresh tomato, you could add 1–2 finely chopped sun-dried tomatoes to the dip.

ROAST AND BRAISED MEAT

You should allow yourself plenty of time for these recipes.

It does take a few hours for a joint of meat to roast in the oven or pot-roast on the stove, or a hearty dish of braised meat or ragout in a sauce to become melt-in-the-mouth tender.

That doesn't necessarily mean more work, however—just a longer waiting time, and you can usefully fill it by preparing side dishes.

In the end, you'll be rewarded with a delicious meal!

ROAST BEEF
with onions, garlic, and mustard

INFO

Horseradish is one of the hottest spices known. If you eat the pure root, you'll get tears in your eyes, but if properly apportioned, horseradish is the perfect companion for many meat, fish, and egg dishes. If you want to add horseradish root to your dishes, make sure you don't cook it with the other ingredients. Horseradish is usually served separately, however: for instance, in the form of horseradish sauce or butter. It can also be combined with apples to make apple and horseradish sauce.

Serves 4

1³/₄ lb (800 g)	beef sirloin
1 large	onion, finely grated
1	crushed garlic clove
1 bunch	parsley, leaves finely chopped
1 tsp	thyme, finely chopped
1 tsp	rosemary, finely chopped
1 tsp	hot mustard
4 tbsp	oil
	Salt
	Pepper

Step by step

Score the layer of fat on the sirloin with a sharp knife in a diamond pattern.

Mix the onion, garlic, and herbs with mustard, 1 tablespoon oil, salt, and pepper.

Preheat the oven to 480 °F/250 °C. Put the rest of the oil in a skillet and brown the meat all over. Spread with the onion and garlic mixture.

Put in a roasting pan, fat side uppermost, reduce the oven temperature to 350 °F/180 °C, and roast for 40 minutes.

Turn off the oven and allow the meat to rest, wrapped in aluminum foil, for 5 minutes.

Side dish

Potatoes—**dauphine potatoes**, for example—are excellent with roast beef. To make, heat $1/2$ cup (125 ml) water with $2\,1/2$ tablespoons (40 g) butter, some salt, and nutmeg, then remove from the heat. Add 5 tablespoons flour, return to the heat, and stir until a lump of dough is formed. Add 4 egg yolks and mashed, cooked potatoes. Use a spoon to form dumpling shapes and deep-fry till golden brown.

Dip

Horseradish sauce is the perfect partner for roast beef. Best of all, use fresh horseradish—about $5\,1/2$ ounces (150 g) for $2/3$ cup (150 ml) heavy whipping cream. Peel the horseradish and grate it finely. Whip the cream until stiff and mix in the horseradish. Season to taste with salt and pepper—and the sauce is ready. Serve the horseradish sauce with slices of roast, sliced as thinly as possible.

SAUCES
for roast beef

Are you still searching for the right sauce for your roast beef? Here, you will find some popular sauces that go well with many of the recipe variations. If you don't have any pan juices to base your sauce on, make a brown stock with a carrot, an onion, a stalk of celery, and meat bouillon.

Bell pepper and peppercorn sauce

Sweat strips of bell pepper and onion rings until soft. If you have pan juices, use these and flakes of butter to make a gravy for the roast, or prepare a brown gravy stock and add pickled green peppercorns. Goes well with the roast beef with onions and garlic, salt crust, Gouda and tomato, and Spanish onions and tomato paste recipe variations.

Honey and mustard sauce

Combine equal parts of honey and coarse-grained Dijon mustard. Add very finely chopped thyme and mix with mayonnaise. Goes well with the salt crust variation.

Gravy with crème fraîche

If you have any meat juices, boil a little water in the skillet to deglaze and pour into a saucepan. Add crème fraîche to the meat juices or brown stock, bring to a boil, and thicken with flour. Season with salt and pepper. Suitable for all recipe variations.

ROAST BEEF
several

The meat will stay particularly juicy if you cook it in the oven with a thick salt crust. This method also makes the meat very tender. If you prefer a crispier crust, we have some tempting suggestions

... with a salt crust

Mix together $5^{1}/_{2}$ oz (150 g) salt and $1^{3}/_{4}$ cups (250 g) flour and stir in water. Allow to rest for 20 minutes in the icebox. Rub the meat with pepper and 2 crushed garlic cloves and cover with 2 sprigs each thyme and rosemary. Roll out the dough and wrap the meat in it. Prick all over with a fork. Roast for 40 minutes at 400 °F/200 °C, reduce the heat to 350 °F/180 °C, and roast for a further 20 minutes.

... with Spanish onions and tomato paste

Season the meat with salt and pepper. Fry over high heat on both sides, then transfer to a roasting pan. Slice $1^{1}/_{4}$ lb (600 g) Spanish onions into rings and cover the meat with them. Heat 1 tablespoon tomato paste in the pan juices with a little water. Pour over the roast beef and cover. Roast for 45–50 minutes at 400 °F/200 °C.

variations

for you here. It is also possible to prepare roast beef as a whole, large joint, in the same way as leg of lamb. Try out the tasty leg of lamb recipes on pages 120–123 with beef!

SAUCES
for roast beef

Hearty sauces with red wine, mustard, apple, or sherry—these sauces are simply delicious!

... with Gouda and tomato

Rub the meat with salt and pepper and place on a roasting rack. Dice 1 red onion and 1 beefsteak tomato and place in a roasting pan. Pour in 1 cup (250 ml) water. Stand the rack in the roasting pan and cook into the oven for 40 minutes at 400 °F/200 °C. Fry 1 finely diced onion until transparent, stir in 7 oz (200 g) grated Gouda, 1 beaten egg, and chopped parsley, and spread on the meat. Bake for a few minutes, until the cheese has melted.

Red wine and cranberry sauce

Roast diced carrots, celeriac, leeks, and onions with the meat (or fry separately from the meat in butter) and pour on red wine and meat stock. Add juniper berries, peppercorns, a bay leaf, rosemary, sour cream, and cranberries. Excellent for roast beef with onions and garlic and for roast beef with a salt crust.

Mustard, cream, and apple sauce

Cook the mustard in the meat juices, or in brown gravy stock, with diced onions and apples. Season to taste with light cream and lemon juice. Excellent for the roast beef with onions and garlic, salt crust, and beef marrow and herbs recipe variations.

... with beef marrow, garlic, and herbs

Purée ³/₄ oz (20 g) beef marrow and 1 clove garlic, and mix with 1 teaspoon each marjoram, rosemary, sage, and thyme. Brush over the meat and chill overnight in plastic wrap. Season with salt and pepper, put in a roasting pan, and sprinkle with 2 tablespoons breadcrumbs. Roast for 40 minutes at 400 °F/200 °C, then allow to rest in the oven for a further 10 minutes at 160 °F/80 °C.

Sherry and cream sauce

Beat eggs with light cream and sherry over medium heat, and allow to reduce a little. Season with nutmeg and salt. Excellent for the roast beef with onions and garlic, salt crust, and beef marrow and herbs recipe variations.

POT-ROAST BEEF
with carrots, leeks, and red wine

Serves 4

2¹/₄ lb (1 kg)	beef (sirloin or round)
	Salt
3 tbsp	oil
3	carrots, coarsely chopped
1 small	leek, coarsely chopped
2	onions, coarsely chopped
1 stalk	celery, coarsely chopped
1 cup (250 ml)	water, bouillon, or red wine
some	peppercorns
1	bay leaf
	Pepper
2 tbsp	flaked butter

INFO

Leeks are in season from June through August and September through December. As a frequently used soup vegetable, they make a tasty ingredient for stews as well. As a vegetable on its own, leek dishes can be prepared in many different ways. Leeks are suitable for blanching, braising, steaming, au gratin recipes, and preserving Always clean whole leeks very carefully, as soil tends to get between the leaves. To do so, slit the stalks from top to bottom, so you can open out the individual layers and wash them out under running water.

Step by step

Wash the meat, pat it dry, and rub with a little salt on all sides.

Heat the oil in a casserole over high heat, add the meat, and brown all over.

Add the carrots, leeks, onions, and celery, and brown with the meat for about 2 minutes.

Add the liquid and seasoning, bring to a boil, cover, and braise over medium heat.

After 1¹/₂ hours, turn the meat and continue to braise for another hour.

Wrap in aluminum foil and keep warm. Add ice-cold flakes of butter to bind the sauce.

Side dish

The classic dish, **red cabbage with apples**, is perfect with pot-roast beef: dice 1 onion and 2 sour apples and sauté in 2 tablespoons lard. Add 1 small red cabbage, cut into strips, 3 tablespoons apple cider vinegar, and ¹/₂ cup (125 ml) apple juice.

Then add 2 cloves and 1 bay leaf and season to taste with salt, pepper, and sugar. Cover and cook over medium heat for about 50 minutes, stirring from time to time. Add more liquid if needed.

INFO

Sometimes it looks **red** and sometimes **blue**, depending on the pH factor of the soil it grows in, but both versions are the same plant: **red cabbage**. It's a firm and crunchy cabbage with reddish-blue, smooth leaves, available almost all the year round. But this cabbage is at its best in the cooler seasons, when hearty meat dishes go down particularly well. Wine, vinegar, or lemon juice make up the characteristic sour component of its flavor, and adding apples or cranberries provides the sweet touch, while other savory ingredients give it its robust taste.

SAUCES
for pot-roast beef

Here we have some suggestions for sauces to go with pot-roasts. The base for all the sauces is the meat juices.

Asian-style sauce

Strain the meat juices from the beef with honey and star anise recipe variation, add bamboo shoots, and bring to a boil. Season to taste with salt and pepper, stir in sesame seeds, and thicken if necessary.

Smooth red wine sauce

Allow sugar to caramelize slightly in clarified butter. Sprinkle in a little flour, and add the meat juices and some of the marinade from the recipe with spiced cookies and ale. Then simmer for 20 minutes with red wine, and add crème fraîche to smooth the sauce.

Easy meat gravy

Strain the meat juices and add some of the vegetable cooking water. Season with salt and pepper. Mix cornstarch with a little water and stir in to thicken the sauce.

... with bacon and spices

Stud the meat with $1^3/_4$ oz (50 g) bacon lardons and brown in a casserole on all sides. Add 3 coarsely chopped carrots, $5^1/_2$ oz (150 g) coarsely diced celery, and 1 sliced leek, together with 3 tablespoons vinegar, peppercorns, allspice, cloves, thyme, and salt. Pour over 2 cups (500 ml) red wine. Cook, covered, over medium heat for $2^1/_2$ hours. Turn the meat during cooking.

... with bacon, tomatoes, and bell pepper

Rub the meat with salt, pepper, and ground paprika. Make a lengthwise cut on the upper side and press in $5^1/_2$ oz (150 g) smoked bacon. Tie the joint with kitchen string and brown all over. Finish cooking in the oven, at 400 °F/200 °C for 90 minutes. Sweat 3 onions cut into rings in butter. Add 4 coarsely diced tomatoes, 1 bell pepper cut into strips, and 8 baby corn. Serve with the joint.

POT-ROAST BEEF
several variations

You can't really braise meat in the oven. In the oven, you use an open roasting pan, but on top of the stove, you braise in a closed casserole.

... with pearl onions and chile

Rub the meat with salt and pepper. Fry on all sides in a casserole and pour off the fat. Melt 3 tablespoons butter in the casserole, turn the meat, add generous 1 lb (500 g) pearl onions, and finely chopped $1/2$ chile. Add salt and roast for 1 hour in the oven with the casserole open, basting from time to time. Add a little finely chopped cilantro.

... with spiced cookies and ale

Marinate the joint for a few days in water, vinegar, 1 each coarsely chopped carrot, celery stalk, and onion, cloves, a bay leaf, peppercorns, allspice, and juniper berries. Fry briefly with 2 tablespoons of marinade, and add 1 cup (250 ml) ale. Braise for 45 minutes, then roast at 350 °F/180 °C for 2 hours. Then add generous $1^{1}/_{2}$ cups (375 ml) ale and 12 crumbled spiced cookies. Cook until done.

... with Worcestershire sauce and Coca-Cola®

Brown the meat on all sides. Mix together salt, 1 tablespoon chile powder,1 teaspoon each thyme, oregano, basil, ground paprika, pepper, chervil, and dry mustard. Pour 1 tablespoon Worcestershire sauce over the meat and scatter the seasoning mix on top. Pour 2 cups (500 ml) Coca-Cola® (not the diet variety) into the pan. Cook in the oven at 375 °F/190 °C for about 30 minutes, then at 300 °F/150 °C for a further 3 hours.

... with honey, star anise, and white wine

Marinate the meat in 4 tablespoons honey, 3 tablespoons soy sauce, 1 tablespoon lemon juice, 2 chopped chiles, 2 each crushed star anise and garlic cloves, salt, and pepper for at least 2 hours. Then brown in a casserole. Braise in the marinade with generous $3/_4$ cup (200 ml) each white wine and beef bouillon over medium heat, for about $2^{1}/_{2}$ hours.

95

ROAST PORK WITH CRACKLING
with carrots, onions, and beer

Serves 4

2¹/₄ lb (1 kg)	*pork joint with skin (Boston Butt, picnic, loin)*
	Salt
3 tbsp	*oil*
3	*carrots, coarsely chopped*
2	*onions, coarsely chopped*
¹/₄	*celeriac root, coarsely chopped*
1 cup (250 ml)	*beer*
1	*bay leaf*
¹/₂ tsp	*rosemary*
2	*cloves*
	Pepper

Step by step

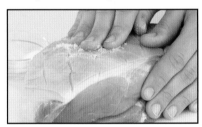

Wash the meat, pat it dry, and rub in a little salt on all sides.

Add the beer, herbs, and spices. Preheat the oven to 400 °F/200 °C.

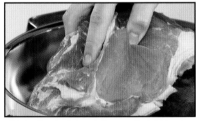

Heat the oil in a roasting pan, add the meat, and brown on all sides. Turn down the heat.

Transfer the meat to the oven and cook for 30 minutes, uncovered. Baste with liquid from time to time.

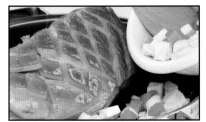

Add the carrots, onions, and celeriac, and brown with the meat for about 2 minutes.

Turn the oven down to 300 °F/150 °C and continue cooking for a further 1 hour.

ROAST MEAT INFO

Crispy crackling is the secret of a really good joint of **roast pork**. With this recipe, you'll succeed! The heat in the oven will coagulate the proteins in the meat, which develops the roasting aromas. But don't forget to keep basting the meat with the liquid, to make sure the skin doesn't dry out. Make diamond-shaped cuts in the **crackling** to

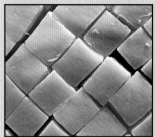

allow the fat to run down over the meat and make a fine base for the gravy.

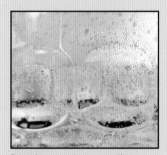

Beer is not only an excellent drink, but a useful ingredient in cooking. Its distinctive flavor is particularly suited to enriching meat dishes, but it can also be an important ingredient in soups and sauces. The many flavors of different types of beer make it possible to vary the recipes individually, ranging from the bitter German Altbier, through sweeter Pilsner-type lagers, to dark, malty ales.

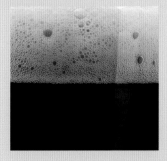

ROAST PORK WITH CRACKLING
several variations

Stuff your roast with delicious ingredients, brush it, add extra ingredients to the pan—this will ensure that the meat is juicy and tender, with a delicious aroma and flavor.

... with dried fruit and cashews

Have the butcher cut a pocket in the joint. Rub the outside and inside with salt and pepper, and stud with cloves. Stuff the pocket with $4^1/_2$ oz (125 g) soaked dried fruit and 3 tablespoons chopped cashews, and close with a skewer. Put the meat in a roasting pan, add 1 cup (250 ml) boiling water, and cook for 2 hours at 300 °F/150 °C. As soon as the meat begins to brown, add 2 cups (500 ml) water and baste frequently.

... with pears, mustard, and white wine

Roast the meat with $^1/_2$ cup (125 ml) water for 10 minutes at 400 °F/200 °C (fat side down). Remove, cut into the skin, stud with cloves, and spread the other side with 1 tablespoon mustard. Roast for $1^1/_2$ hours. Halve generous 1 lb (500 g) pears and stud each half with a clove. Sauté with 1 tablespoon butter, $^1/_2$ cup (125 ml) white wine, 1 teaspoon sugar, a bay leaf, and pepper for 15 minutes, then serve with the meat.

... with cinnamon, shallots, and apple wine

Score the skin of the joint and stud with cloves. Spread the meat with 1 tablespoon cinnamon, salt, pepper, and allspice mixed with 1 tablespoon honey, and marinate for 1 hour. Brown the meat and add 12 whole, peeled shallots. Pour on $^2/_3$ cup (150 ml) apple wine. Cover and cook for 90 minutes at 300 °F/150 °C, sprinkle with 1 tablespoon superfine sugar after 45 minutes, and continue to roast uncovered.

... with onions and ale

Rub the meat on all sides with salt, pepper, marjoram, and 1 crushed clove garlic. Brown on all sides in a casserole. Add 2 cups (500 ml) meat bouillon and 2 cups (500 ml) ale. Add 20 small, whole onions and simmer for about 2 hours. Remove the meat and onions from the casserole, strain the cooking juices, and reduce a little.

SIDE DISHES
for roast pork

Pork is a very popular roast, with many ways of serving potatoes as an accompaniment— including the classic potatoes cooked in their skins below. Or simply serve with peeled and boiled potatoes.

Potatoes in their skins with chives
Thoroughly scrub non-mealy potatoes with a vegetable brush under running water. Boil for about 20 minutes in plenty of salt water, drain, and scatter with chives.

... with pineapple, ketchup, and vinegar
Rub the meat with salt and pepper. Sauté 2 diced onions in 1 tablespoon oil in a roasting pan, add the meat, and roast for about 1$^1/_2$ hours at 300 °F/150 °C. Mix together 7 tablespoons (100 ml) vinegar, 2 tablespoons each sugar and ketchup, 1 tablespoon bouillon, 3$^1/_2$ oz (100 g) pineapple in juice, and 1 tablespoon cornstarch. Deglaze the pan with water, strain, add the pineapple mixture, and bring to a boil, stirring continuously.

... with herbs, whole grain mustard, and thyme
Season the meat with salt and pepper and transfer to a roasting pan with 1 coarsely chopped carrot, onion, and celery stalk. Pour over 3 tablespoons melted clarified butter. Cook for 1$^1/_2$ hours at 300 °F/150 °C. After about 30 minutes, pour over 2 cups (500 ml) water. Mix 2 tablespoons each thyme and oregano with 2 tablespoons honey and 1 tablespoon each hot and whole grain mustard. Spread over the meat 30 minutes before the end of cooking.

Boiled potatoes
Peel the potatoes, wash, then halve or quarter them. Put in a pan, cover halfway up with water, add salt, and boil for about 15–20 minutes until done. After cooking, leave to stand, uncovered, with the heat turned off to allow the steam to escape.

MUSTARD INFO

Mustard is made from the seeds of the white, brown, or black mustard plant. The whole seeds are used. Ground seeds are often used for mustard powder, but mainly the seeds are used to form the spicy paste of ready-made mustard. There are innumerable varieties, differing in the blend of types of mustard, the fineness of the grains, the

vinegar added, and other ingredients such as sugar, caramel, honey, horseradish, cayenne, herbs and spices, lemon juice, wine, garlic, tomato, or paprika. Medium-hot mustard is mainly made from white and brown mustard seeds, with horseradish sometimes added to make horseradish mustard. Hot mustard has a higher proportion

of hot mustard seeds, mild mustard consists of coarsely ground, partly roasted mustard seeds, and sweet mustard has sugar, sweeteners, or honey added to it. In the coarser, whole grain mustards, whole seeds with their husks are used. Dijon mustard must be made from brown mustard seeds, peeled in a special process and without the mustard oil being removed.

Serves 4

4	beef steaks (about 5¹/₂ oz/150 g each)
	Salt
	Pepper
8	rashers bacon
4 tsp	mustard
2	onions, sliced into rings
2	gherkins, halved lengthwise
	Toothpicks
	Flour
2 tbsp	oil
¹/₂ cup (125 ml)	stock

Step by step

Press the steaks flat with your hands and season with salt and pepper.

Fry well in 2 tablespoons oil on all sides, for several minutes.

Spread 2 bacon rashers, 1 teaspoon mustard, ¹/₂ onion in rings, and ¹/₂ gherkin on each steak, leaving a border.

Half fill the pan with stock, cover, and braise for 1¹/₂ hours.

Roll up each steak and fasten with a toothpick, or tie with kitchen string. Coat in flour.

Remove the toothpick or kitchen string before serving.

BEEF OLIVES
with bacon, gherkins, and mustard

SIDE DISHES
for beef olives

Creamy vegetable dishes are best with hearty, savory beef olives. Here are two suitable suggestions:

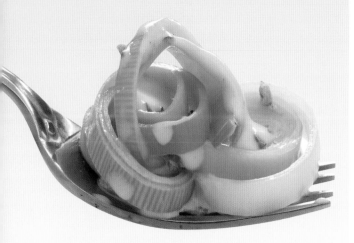

Leeks in cream sauce

Cut leeks in sections about 1 in. (3 cm) long and sweat in butter or oil. Season lightly with salt. Add a little water—just enough to stop the leeks sticking to the bottom of the pan. Simmer until almost soft, add light cream, and reduce slightly. Season to taste with nutmeg.

Creamed spinach

Blanch spinach in saltwater, drain well, and chop. Sweat diced shallots until transparent, add light cream, and reduce to thicken. Stir in the spinach and season to taste with salt, pepper, and nutmeg.

BEEF OLIVES
several

A great invention: cover thin slices of meat with ingredients to taste, roll them up, and fry or braise them. There you have a popular meat dish with a surprise inside. Let your imagination run free, because there are innumerable options for beef

... with sauerkraut, bell peppers, and green olives

Cut 1 red bell pepper into strips. To fill 1 beef olive, take one-quarter of the bell pepper strips, 2 tablespoons each sauerkraut and finely chopped, pitted green olives, and salt. Spread on the steak. Roll up the meat, secure, coat in flour, and fry; then cover with stock and braise.

... with Feta, pepperoncini, and garlic

Season the meat with salt, pepper, and sweet paprika. To fill 1 beef olive, take $1/_2$ mild pepperoncini, 2 tablespoons chopped Feta, and 1 clove garlic, and spread over the meat. Roll up, secure, coat in flour, and fry; then cover with stock and braise.

SIDE DISHES
for beef olives

olive fillings. Take care to fasten the beef olives with toothpicks or kitchen string, to prevent them unrolling during the cooking process!

The fresh taste of cucumbers and chervil makes a lovely contrast to beef olives. And in the mushroom season, serve bolete in cream sauce with beef olives—a special treat!

... with spinach, Emmental, and sage

Blanch about 3 oz (80 g) spinach. To fill 1 beef olive, take $^1/_4$ spinach together with 1 slice cured ham, 1 slice Emmental, 1 small clove garlic, a little salt, pepper, and 2 sage leaves. Spread on the meat. Roll up, secure, coat in flour, and fry; then cover with stock and braise.

Bolete in cream sauce

Halve, quarter, or slice the mushrooms, according to size. Drizzle over some lemon juice. Sweat diced onions in butter, add the mushrooms, and cook for a few minutes. Season with salt and pepper. Stir flour into light cream, heat, and add half-and-half cream until desired consistency is achieved. Stir in the mushrooms.

... with apple and cured ham

Peel 2 apples, core them, and cut into wedges. Finely dice 1 onion and chop $^1/_2$ bunch parsley. To fill 1 beef olive, place $^1/_2$ slice cured ham, $^1/_4$ apple in wedges, $^1/_4$ diced onion, and $^1/_4$ chopped parsley on each steak. Roll up, secure, and braise in a casserole with 9 oz (250 g) quartered tomatoes and the remaining apple wedges.

Cucumbers in chervil cream

Peel the cucumbers, deseed, and slice about 1 in. (2 cm) thick. Sweat diced onion in butter until golden yellow, add the cucumbers, and simmer for about 10 minutes until al dente. Remove from the heat. Stir in half-and-half cream, crushed garlic, and pepper. Add the cucumbers in the butter. Thicken with cornstarch blended with a little water, and sprinkle with chopped chervil.

CURED AND SMOKED PORK LOIN
with celery, leeks, carrots, and onions

Serves 4

11 oz (300 g)	*casserole vegetables (onion, celery, leeks, carrots)*
2 tbsp	*oil*
1¹/₄ cups (300 ml)	*bouillon*
1	*bay leaf*
5	*cloves*
10	*black peppercorns*
10	*mustard seeds*
2	*lovage stems (or celery stalks)*
2¹/₄ lb (1 kg)	*boned smoked pork loin*
3¹/₂ oz (100 g)	*red onions*
4 tbsp	*butter*

INFO

Casserole vegetables, prepacked vegetable combinations for casseroles, stews, soups, and stock are widely available, both fresh and frozen. The best mixtures combine carrots, leeks, and root vegetables such as parsnips; you can recreate these or vary them, and add other ingredients, such as parsley. If using the vegetables for soups, they can be chopped small and eaten with the soup, or used whole and removed from the stock after cooking. In braised dishes, they are first fried or roasted, then cooked to make a creamy sauce.

Step by step

Dice the vegetables and fry in the oil in a large casserole. Add the bouillon, herbs, and spices, and the lovage.

Score the pork loin on the fat side and place on top of the vegetable mix.

Cook the meat in a preheated oven at 375 °F/190 °C, covered, for about 60 minutes, basting every 10 minutes with the stock.

Remove the meat from the casserole and keep warm. Strain the meat juices and reduce by one-third.

Dice the red onions and sweat in 2 tablespoons butter until transparent. Bind the gravy with 2 tablespoons ice-cold butter flakes.

Add the red onions plus the pieces of carrot and leek from the meat juices.

INFO

Sauerkraut is made from thinly sliced white cabbage fermented in barrels with salt. During fermentation, lactic acid develops, which has many positive health qualities. It is good for the digestion and the stomach, and even fights bacteria. Because of its high vitamin C content, sauerkraut was highly esteemed in the past when there were few sources of fresh foods providing vitamins in the winter. Sailors ate it to protect themselves from the feared disease caused by vitamin C deficiency, scurvy. Fresh sauerkraut has a milder flavor than bottled sauerkraut.

Side dish

For a savory pork loin dish, sauerkraut is essential. Sweat 1 diced onion with 1 tablespoon sugar and 1 quartered apple in 4 tablespoons (60 g) butter. Gradually add 1³/₄ lb (750 g) sauerkraut (fresh or from a jar) and simmer for 10 minutes, stirring repeatedly. Cook fresh sauerkraut with 5 juniper berries, 1 bay leaf, and a little water for about 1 hour. Sauerkraut from a jar needs only 20–30 minutes.

SIDE DISHES
for smoked pork loin

What could be better with smoked pork loin than various kinds of dumplings? Made with raw or cooked potatoes, or with bread rolls and bacon, they are always the perfect partner.

Boiled dumplings
Peel and boil $2^1/_4$ lb (1 kg) mealy potatoes. Push through a ricer. Mix with generous 1 cup (150 g) all-purpose flour, salt, nutmeg, and 2 eggs. Shape into dumplings and stuff each with toasted cubes of bread roll. Place in boiling salt water, reduce the heat, and simmer for about 20 minutes.

Bread dumplings with bacon
Dice 6 stale bread rolls and soak for 30 minutes in a mixture of 1 cup (250 ml) milk, 5 eggs, and salt. Sweat diced onion and chopped parsley in butter and add to the bread rolls with $4^1/_2$ oz (125 g) diced bacon. Bind with a little flour if required and leave to stand. Shape into dumplings. Simmer for 20 minutes in salt water.

CURED AND SMOKED
several

Cured and smoked pork loin cuts can be quite salty so, if you are using this type of meat, be careful with the salt! Also, curing and smoking makes the meat rather crumbly, so it needs less cooking time than other joints. If you cook it for too long, the meat will become dry. The salty and smoky flavor goes best

... with onions, apples, and sour cream
Brown the pork loin. Add 3 quartered onions and 1 quartered apple and pour on 8 cups (2 l) meat bouillon. Simmer for 1 hour with 2 teaspoons caraway. Remove the apples, onions, and meat. Reduce the meat stock and adjust the seasoning. Bind the sauce with $^1/_2$ cup (125 ml) sour cream. Return the apples and onions to the sauce.

... with pineapple and leeks
Make 8 x $^1/_2$-in. (1-cm) deep cuts in the pork loin and place $^1/_2$ canned pineapple ring in each. Cook in the oven with $^1/_2$ cup (125 ml) bouillon at 400 °F/200 °C for about 1 hour. Slice 2 leeks into rings, finely dice 1 onion, and sweat together in 1 tablespoon oil. Braise for about 5 minutes with 1 cup (250 ml) sour cream, bind the sauce, and season with salt and nutmeg. Serve with the pork loin.

PORK LOIN
variations

with sweet and sour ingredients, such as apples or pineapple. An absolute classic side dish for smoked pork loin is sauerkraut, but as well as serving it as a side dish, you can cook it together with the meat.

SIDE DISHES
for smoked pork loin

Peas or beans—both these members of the legume family have a strong individual taste, making them well suited to the savory pork loin.

Buttered peas

Sweat fresh peas in butter, then add bouillon, salt, and pepper, and simmer for about 10 minutes until soft. Stir in butter to serve.

... with sausage meat stuffing

Hollow the pork loin out a little. Dice the cut-out pieces of pork loin and mix with 7 oz (200 g) sausage meat, 1 finely chopped onion, 1 tablespoon chopped parsley, $^1/_2$ teaspoon each marjoram and thyme, salt, pepper, and 1 egg. Stuff the meat with the mixture. Brush with oil and rub with 1 teaspoon sweet paprika. Cover the opening in the meat with aluminum foil. Roast in the oven for 45 minutes at 400 °F/200 °C.

... with an onion and mustard crust

Rub the pork loin with 1 teaspoon pepper and cook in a casserole with $1^1/_4$ cups (300 ml) water for 45 minutes at 400 °F/200 °C. To make the crust, dice 7 oz (200 g) Spanish onions and sweat in butter until transparent. Crumble 2 slices toast and mix with the onions and 3 tablespoons medium-hot mustard to form a paste. Remove the pork loin, spread the mixture over it, and roast for a further 45 minutes.

Fava beans with bacon

Remove the fava beans from their pods and cook with summer savory in salt water for 20 minutes. Fry some diced bacon in oil until crisp then sauté sliced scallions in the bacon fat. Add the drained fava beans and simmer for 5 minutes. Sprinkle with chopped mixed herbs.

107

MEAT RAGOUT
with Spanish onions

INFO

The term **"ragout"** refers to a dish consisting of braised or stewed pieces of meat, fish, or mushrooms and other ingredients, cooked in a usually creamy and spicy sauce. Because it needs a longer cooking time, meat has to be (pre-)cooked separately from the other ingredients at the beginning, while fast-cooking pieces of fish are dropped into the sauce toward the end as they only need to simmer for a few minutes.

Serves 4

1¹/₄ lb (600 g)	*pork or beef (brisket or plate), diced*
6 tbsp	*oil*
1³/₄ lb (750 g)	*onions, halved and sliced*
2 tsp	*tomato paste*
2 tsp	*hot paprika*
2 tsp	*sweet paprika*
2 tbsp	*red wine*
generous ¹/₄ cup (200 ml)	*meat bouillon*
	Salt
	Ground caraway

Step by step

Fry the meat in batches, in 3 tablespoons of oil. Keep warm.

Heat 3 tablespoons of oil in a skillet and sweat the onions, stirring continuously.

Add the tomato paste and mix well.

Sprinkle the paprika on the onions, allow it to bubble, and immediately pour on the red wine and bouillon.

Add the meat, season with salt and caraway, and mix well. Braise for about 1 hour over low heat.

Side dish

The dough for **Spätzle**—a German form of pasta and typical accompaniment for ragout—is very easy to make. However, scraping off the slivers of dough if you don't have a scraper is harder. Mix 3 cups (400 g) flour, 4 eggs, about $^1/_2$ cup (125 ml) water, and 1 teaspoon salt to make a viscous dough and let it rest for 10 minutes. Then, in a large saucepan, bring enough salt water to a boil and press the dough in batches through a ricer into the boiling water. Remove with a slotted spoon.

Side dish

Brussels sprouts make a delicious side dish for this meal. Thoroughly clean $1^3/_4$ lb (750 g) Brussels sprouts and cut a small cross in the stem of each. Pour on 1 cup (250 ml) vegetable bouillon and simmer for 10 minutes until soft. Season to taste with salt, pepper, and nutmeg, and dot with 2 tablespoons butter flakes.

SIDE DISHES
for meat ragout

You can always serve plain rice with a meat ragout. Or just add a little more pizzazz to parboiled rice.

Buttered rice

Sweat ³/₄ cup (150 g) rice with diced onion in butter until transparent. Pour on double the quantity of bouillon and add salt. Allow to simmer for 20 minutes, then stir in flakes of butter.

Zucchini rice

Sweat ³/₄ cup (150 g) rice with diced onion in butter until transparent. Pour on double the quantity of bouillon and add salt. Allow to simmer for 20 minutes. Stir in grated, sautéed zucchini and grated Gouda.

"Risi e bisi"

Sweat ³/₄ cup (150 g) rice with diced onions in butter until transparent and pour on double the quantity of bouillon. Add frozen peas and salt. Simmer over low heat for 20 minutes.

... with green bell pepper, tomatoes, and onions

Brown the meat over high heat, season with salt and pepper, and remove from the pan. Then sweat 2 chopped onions and 1 crushed garlic clove, sprinkle with ground paprika, and add the meat. Reduce the liquid, then cover with 2 cups (500 ml) water and cook for 1 hour. Sauté 1 sliced onion, 1 green bell pepper, cut into strips, and 2 quartered tomatoes, add to the meat, and cook for a further 20 minutes.

... with red bell peppers and green beans

Brown the meat over high heat and remove from the pan. Sauté 1 coarsely diced Spanish onion with 3 tablespoons tomato paste. Add the meat and season with salt and pepper. Cover with 2 cups (500 ml) bouillon and cook for about 1 hour. Add 5¹/₂ oz (150 g) cooked green beans and 2 red bell peppers, cut into strips, and cook for a further 5 minutes. Season to taste with 2 tablespoons ketchup, salt, and pepper.

MEAT RAGOUT
several variations

Characteristic flavorings and ingredients for meat ragouts include onions, paprika, caraway, and garlic. Here you can find recipes both classic and unusual that you can prepare with the meat of your choice.

... with sauerkraut, shallots, and sour cream

Sweat 7 oz (200 g) diced shallots and 2 crushed garlic cloves, and dust with 2 tablespoons ground paprika. Add the meat, brown, and season with salt, sugar, and caraway. Add a bay leaf and stir in 1 tablespoon tomato paste. Mix in generous 1 lb (500 g) sauerkraut, add just enough water to cover, and cook for 1 hour. Finish by stirring in $1/2$ cup (125 ml) sour cream.

... with red wine, plums, and ginger

Marinate the meat for 3 hours in 4 tablespoons each oil and soy sauce, the juice of 1 lemon, 1 piece ginger, and 2 tablespoons brown sugar. Brown the meat over high heat and season with salt and pepper. Combine in a casserole with 12 sweet plums, 7 tablespoons (100 ml) game bouillon, $1^2/_3$ cups (400 ml) red wine, 2 teaspoons mustard, and 6 teaspoons plum purée. Cook, in a covered casserole, at 400 °F/200 °C for about 1 hour. Add light cream and season with salt and pepper.

... with coffee and aquavit

Brown the meat, in batches, in 3 tablespoons butter over high heat. Add 1 teaspoon salt, pepper, 2 tablespoons strong coffee, 3 tablespoons light cream, 2 tablespoons tomato paste, and 1 teaspoon aquavit. Simmer for about 1 hour over low heat.

... with coconut milk, pineapple, and curry powder

Brown the meat over high heat and pour over 2 cups (500 ml) bouillon. Braise for 1 hour at 400 °F/200 °C. Thirty minutes before the end of cooking time, add $5^1/_2$ oz (150 g) pineapple cubes, 2 teaspoons curry powder, 3 tablespoons coconut milk, 7 tablespoons (100 ml) light cream, and salt. Thicken a little if required.

PORK TENDERLOIN

PORK TENDERLOIN
with carrots and meat bouillon

Serves 4

1½ lb (600 g)	pork tenderloin
	Salt
	Pepper
4 tbsp	oil
½	onion, sliced into rings
1	carrot, cut into strips
1	tomato, skinned and quartered
1 cup (250 ml)	meat bouillon
1	bay leaf
1 sprig	rosemary
1 sprig	thyme

Step by step

Remove the skin and sinews from the tenderloin and rub with salt and pepper.

Braise, covered, for 20 minutes. Add a little more bouillon if required.

Heat the oil in a pan, add the meat, and brown all over.

Remove the meat from the stock and keep warm.

Add the onion, carrot, and tomato to the pan, pour on half the meat bouillon, and season with the herbs.

Strain the stock, reduce briefly, and adjust seasoning to taste.

STOCK INFO

Stock is the foundation of many soups and sauces and acts as a cooking liquid for meat, poultry, fish, and vegetables. It consists of water enriched with the flavors, minerals, and fat of food that has been cooked in it. As the stock already adds flavoring and minerals that are partially absorbed by the ingredients being cooked in it, any food cooked in stock is enriched in

flavor. You can make stock with vegetables, bones, meat, poultry, or fish, or any combination of these, depending on the intended use. To make sure the stock is particularly tasty and aromatic, the ingredients are put in cold water and cooked in an uncovered pan, with salt added only toward the end of the cooking time. The scum of coagulated protein that forms is removed, and after 2–3 hours' cooking the stock is clarified. To do this, bring beaten egg white to a boil in the previously strained stock. This will coagulate and bind the floating bodies to itself. The stock is then filtered and, if necessary, any fat is skimmed off.

The aromatic leaves of the **bay** tree always go well with veal and beef, and they are often also used for Sauerbraten (German-style marinated beef), fricassee, poultry, game, pies and pâtés, ragouts, red cabbage, soups, and stews.

PORK TENDERLOIN
several variations

The following recipes will give you some idea of how versatile pork tenderloin is. The range of flavors extends from mild and tasty with tomatoes, baby carrots, or cream, to a hearty country style with beer and caraway.

... with parsley root and white wine

Rub the meat with salt, pepper, and rosemary. Cut $1/2$ red onion into strips and 1 parsley root into slices. Brown the meat, then sweat with the onion and parsley root. Pour on 3 tablespoons white wine, add $1/2$ cup (125 ml) bouillon and $1/2$ bay leaf, and braise, covered, at 400 °F/200 °C for 15 minutes. Remove the meat and deglaze the pot with $1/2$ cup (125 ml) stock. Strain, and reduce.

... with pepper and cream

Mix 1 tablespoon black pepper and 1 teaspoon cayenne with 1 tablespoon sweet paprika, 1 teaspoon salt, and 2 tablespoons oil. Rub the pork tenderloin with this mixture. Brown in a skillet on all sides. Transfer the meat to a roasting pan and roast for 15 minutes at 400 °F/200 °C. Brown 1 finely diced onion in the skillet juices and reduce with $1^2/3$ cup (400 ml) light cream. Serve the sauce with the meat.

...with beer, caraway, and whole grain mustard

Marinate the tenderloin for 24 hours in generous $3/4$ cup (200 ml) oil, 4 cups (1 liter) Pilsner, $1/2$ each diced carrot, leek, and celery stalk, 2 bay leaves, 6 cloves, 1 teaspoon juniper berries, 2 teaspoons crushed peppercorns, and salt. Mix 14 oz (400 g) diced white bread, 1 egg, 2 teaspoons caraway, 7 oz (200 g) mustard, 2 eggs, generous $3/4$ cup (200 ml) ale, pepper, and salt. Pour over the pork tenderloin and roast for 15 minutes at 400 °F/200 °C. Serve with the beer sauce.

... with ginger, chilli sauce, and peaches

Rub the pork tenderloin with thyme, rosemary, and pepper and leave to soak in. Season the meat with salt, brown in a skillet, then roast for 15 minutes at 400 °F/200 °C. Sweat 2 diced onions, 1 teaspoon curry powder, 1 tablespoon ginger syrup (from a jar), 6 tablespoons chilli sauce, and 6 tablespoons soy sauce with 2 chopped pieces of ginger from the jar. Pour on generous $3/4$ cup (200 ml) light cream and simmer. Add 4 canned peach quarters to the pork. Serve with the sauce.

SIDE DISHES
for pork tenderloin

Country potato wedges, rösti, or croquettes: deep or pan-fried potatoes are very popular and their aromatic roasted flavor is excellent with tasty meat dishes.

Country potato wedges

Peel the potatoes and cut into wedges. Deep fry for 15 minutes in hot fat at 300 °F/150 °C, increase the deep-fryer temperature to 350 °F/180 °C, and continue frying for 3–5 minutes until crisp. Drain, and season with salt.

Rösti

Cook potatoes in their skins and allow to stand overnight. Peel, grate roughly, and season with salt. Brown in butter, push the potato mass together, and press down with a spatula. Cover and fry over low heat until golden brown. Tip the potatoes out into the lid, melt butter in the pan, slide the rösti into the pan, and fry until golden brown on the second side.

... with green bell pepper, tomatoes, and scallions

Rub the meat on all sides with salt, pepper, and 1 crushed clove garlic. Brown on all sides in 3 tablespoons butter, then remove from the pan. Sweat 3 sliced scallions and 2 quartered green bell peppers in the pan juices and add 3 quartered tomatoes. Simmer briefly. Season with salt, paprika, and thyme, then add $^1/_2$ bunch chopped parsley. Return the meat to the pan and braise, covered, for 20 minutes.

Potato croquettes

Push boiled mealy potatoes through a ricer while they are still hot. Mix with butter, egg yolk, salt, and nutmeg. Shape into a roll and cut into small cylinders. Coat in dried breadcrumbs and deep fry in hot fat.

... with Parma ham and baby carrots

Cover the pork tenderloin with parsley and wrap in 4 slices Parma ham. Brown all over and season with salt and pepper. Roast for about 15 minutes at 400 °F/200 °C. Cook $2^1/_4$ lb (1 kg) baby carrots for 12 minutes with a pinch of sugar. Heat 1 cup (250 ml) hollandaise sauce, stir in some chopped parsley, and season to taste with pepper and 1 tablespoon orange juice. Serve with the meat.

MUSHROOM INFO

Common-store mushrooms are also known as white button mushrooms, Italian brown mushrooms, and market mushrooms, among many other names. They belong to the order of gilled mushrooms, which means they have gills on the underside of the cap, ranging in color from whitish to dark brown, depending on the age of

the mushroom. When you buy, look out for closed caps, a sign of young mushrooms.

Large mushrooms with open caps and dark gills are older. The best-known wild mushroom is the common field mushroom, a close relative of the cultivated mushroom. There are also aromatic anise mushrooms, which have a wonderful scent, such as horse mushrooms.

Cultivated common-store mushrooms are grown on fermented horse dung and are economically the most important edible mushrooms in Europe and North America. White and brown varieties are available, but the difference in flavor is hardly discernible. Larger mushrooms are excellent for stuffing. Do take care if you forage for your own mushrooms. It's possible, when looking for some varieties, to confuse them with the poisonous ones!

Serves 4

1¹/₂ lb (600 g)	pork or veal (round cut)
2 tbsp	flour
3 tbsp	oil
	Salt
	Pepper
3 tbsp	butter
1 small	onion, finely diced
¹/₂ cup (125 ml)	dry white wine
7 oz (200 g)	sliced mushrooms
¹/₂ cup (125 ml)	bouillon
³/₄ cup (200 ml)	light cream

Step by step

Cut the meat into strips. Dust with a little flour, ensuring it is evenly coated.

Melt the butter in a skillet, sweat the onions, pour over the wine, and reduce. Briefly sauté the mushrooms with the onions.

Briefly fry the meat in batches in the oil, stirring well. It should not be allowed to color.

Add the bouillon and cream, reduce, and season to taste with salt and pepper.

Season the individual batches with salt and pepper, and keep warm.

Add the meat to the sauce and heat.

GESCHNETZELTES
with white wine, mushrooms, and cream

SIDE DISHES
for geschnetzeltes

Rice and couscous make wonderful side dishes for geschnetzeltes!

Couscous with vegetables

Sweat 9 oz (250 g) couscous in 1 tablespoon butter. Pour on 1$\frac{1}{2}$ cups (375 ml) water or vegetable bouillon, bring to a boil, and simmer for 15 minutes. Lightly sauté $\frac{1}{2}$ bunch chopped scallions in oil with 1 each diced red and yellow bell pepper. Stir into the couscous. Season with salt and pepper.

Djuvec rice

Simmer 9 oz (250 g) rice in 2 cups (500 ml) water for 20 minutes. Slice 1 leek into rings and sweat in oil with 1 crushed garlic clove and $\frac{1}{2}$ each chopped red, green, and yellow bell pepper. Simmer 4 diced tomatoes with the peppers, garlic, and leek. Mix with the rice and season with salt, pepper, and paprika.

Pilau rice

Sweat 1 chopped onion in oil with 9 oz (250 g) rice. Pour on 2 cups (500 ml) bouillon and simmer for 20 minutes. Stir in chopped parsley, finely chopped chiles, salt, pepper, and butter flakes.

... with tomatoes, cucumber, and lentils

Brown the meat with 4 diced onions. Dust with 3 tablespoons curry powder and cook for 2–3 minutes. Add 14 oz (400 g) whole canned tomatoes with the juice and simmer briefly. Add 2 cups (500 ml) bouillon, cover, and cook over medium heat for 10 minutes. Heat 9 oz (250 g) canned lentils and add to the meat mixture with $\frac{1}{2}$ peeled and grated cucumber and $\frac{1}{2}$ teaspoon sambal ulek paste.

... with green bell peppers and Chinese cabbage

Brown the meat briefly in batches, season with salt and pepper, and remove from the pan. Fry 2 green bell peppers cut into strips for 2–3 minutes, and season with sambal ulek paste and ground paprika. Briefly simmer 1 tablespoon tomato paste with the mixture. Add 14 ounces (400 g) Chinese (napa) cabbage, cut into strips, add 1 tablespoon oyster sauce in generous $\frac{3}{4}$ cup (200 ml) water, and cook over medium heat for 15 minutes. Serve with $\frac{1}{2}$ bunch chopped chervil.

GESCHNETZELTES
several variations

In the same way as ragout, geschnetzeltes is first fried and then cooked in a sauce that is reduced until thickened. Here are a few popular variations; you can alter them to suit your own taste.

... with curry powder, crème fraîche, and yogurt

Briefly brown the meat in batches. Add 2 diced onions and fry with the meat, then season with salt and pepper. Add 2 tablespoons each flour, curry powder, and tomato paste, and heat briefly with the other ingredients. Pour on 2 cups (500 ml) bouillon and simmer for 15 minutes. Add $5^1/_2$ oz (150 g) crème fraîche and $3^1/_2$ oz (100 g) yogurt, and heat briefly.

... with mixed mushrooms, sweet corn, and Gouda

Brown the meat in batches and keep warm. Sweat 1 diced onion in the pan, sprinkle over 2 tablespoons flour, add a little bouillon, and simmer for 10 minutes. Add the meat, $5^1/_2$ oz (150 g) mixed mushrooms, and $3^1/_2$ oz (100 g) canned sweet corn. Stir in $^1/_2$ cup (125 ml) light cream and season to taste with salt, pepper, and lemon juice. Place in an ovenproof dish, sprinkle with 7 oz (200 g) grated Gouda, and bake at 400 °F/200 °C until the cheese has melted.

... with peas, celeriac, and leeks

Briefly brown the meat in batches. Season with salt, pepper, paprika, and 1 tablespoon Worcestershire sauce, and continue to cook for 5 minutes. Fry 2 leeks, sliced into rings, and $^1/_2$ celeriac, cut into sticks, and add to the meat. Add 7 oz (200 g) peas and 1 cup (250 ml) each Pilsner and bouillon to the meat and vegetables. Simmer for 5–10 minutes and finish with $^1/_2$ cup (125 ml) sour cream.

... with apples, red onions, and honey

Brown the meat in batches and keep warm. Sweat 1 diced red onion in butter in the skillet until transparent. Add 2 diced apples and 1 teaspoon honey, and caramelize lightly. Pour on $^1/_2$ cup (125 ml) white wine, 1 cup (250 ml) beef bouillon, and $^1/_2$ cup (125 ml) apple juice, return the meat to the pan, and simmer for 15 minutes. Stir in 7 oz (200 g) crème fraîche and season with marjoram.

LEG OF LAMB
with white wine and parsley

Serves 4

1	*leg of lamb (about 3 lb/1.4 kg) on the bone*
2 sprigs	*rosemary*
3	*garlic cloves, 1 crushed*
	Salt
	Pepper
9 tbsp	*butter*
¹/₂ cup (125 ml)	*white wine*
2	*egg yolks*
1 bunch	*parsley*
3–4 tbsp	*breadcrumbs*
2 cups (500 ml)	*bouillon*
1 tsp	*cornstarch*

Step by step

Remove the fat and skin from the lamb and loosen the meat from the bone. Slide in the rosemary and whole garlic cloves. Season with salt and pepper.

Mix the egg yolks, parsley, crushed garlic clove, and breadcrumbs with the butter.

Brown in a roasting pan with 5 tablespoons butter, then roast in the oven at 160–200 °F/80–100 °C for about 5 hours, or at 350 °F/180 °C for 1 hour.

Remove the leg of lamb and deglaze the pan with the bouillon. Strain, add to the egg mixture, and bind the sauce with cornstarch. Brush the leg of lamb with parsley butter.

Baste the leg of lamb with the wine and pan juices from time to time. Beat the remaining butter until it foams.

Broil the leg of lamb on the lower shelf for 8 minutes, switch off the broiler, and leave to rest for 10 minutes. Serve with the sauce.

ROSEMARY INFO

Lamb and **rosemary** are the perfect culinary combination. Before it became popular in the kitchen, rosemary was used in religious practices and for medicinal purposes. But it also has plenty to offer the cook: it is an excellent partner for meat

dishes, particularly lamb, and for potatoes. Rosemary is a vital ingredient in Mediterranean cooking (especially in Italy and the Provence region of France).

GARLIC INFO

Garlic is the perfect partner for spring lamb, lamb, and mutton. It may also scare off vampires! Garlic can be used in both cold and hot dishes but, if you fry it, take care not to let it brown too deeply, as it will quickly become

bitter. Garlic may make food taste delicious, but many people find the odors exuded by those who have eaten it highly unpleasant. Recommended counter-measures may be more or less effective: chewing cardamom seeds or parsley, or drinking milk. In some parts of Austria, garlic is also known as the "poor man's (or woman's) vanilla." The "vanilla roast" in those regions is accordingly not seasoned with vanilla, but with garlic.

LEG OF LAMB
several variations

Lamb is far more popular in Mediterranean regions than it is in more northerly countries. These recipes, which accentuate its mild flavor, will hopefully encourage people to serve it more often.

... with red wine, cumin, and cinnamon

Make a purée with 3 cloves garlic, 1 onion, salt, pepper, cinnamon, $1/2$ teaspoon cumin, $1/2$ bunch parsley, rosemary, 1 tablespoon lemon juice, and 4 tablespoons olive oil. Bone the leg of lamb, shape into a roll, and secure with string. Marinate for 4 hours. Brown in a roasting pan and roast with $1/2$ cup (125 ml) red wine for 20 minutes at 400 °F/200 °C, then for 40 minutes at 325 °F/160 °C.

... with garlic and sherry

Insert 6 quartered garlic cloves under the skin. Brush with salt, pepper, rosemary, and oil, and marinate for 4 hours. Pour over 6 tablespoons melted butter and roast for 1 hour at 350 °F/180 °C. Baste from time to time with the pan juices and additional bouillon. Remove the leg of lamb and deglaze the pan with bouillon. Add 2 tablespoons sherry, reduce, and finish with 2 tablespoons crème fraîche.

... with kidney beans, tomatoes, and sweet corn

Stud the leg of lamb with 4 cloves slivered garlic. Mix 1 tablespoon each thyme, rosemary and oregano with 2 tablespoons olive oil and rub over the leg of lamb. Season with salt, then brown all over. Add 14 oz (400 g) canned tomatoes and 1 cup (250 ml) red wine. Cover and braise for about 1 hour. Heat $51/2$ oz (150 g) canned kidney beans with $13/4$ oz (50 g) canned sweet corn and add to the braised lamb. Season with salt and pepper.

... with green bell peppers, honey, and saffron

Rub the leg of lamb with salt. Lightly fry 2 finely chopped onions and 2 green bell peppers in a little oil. Add the leg of lamb and brown all over. Add $1/4$ oz (5 g) saffron, 1 tablespoon brandy, generous $3/4$ cup (200 ml) white wine, and $1/2$ teaspoon paprika. Cook for 10 minutes, cover the leg of lamb with water, and braise for 40 minutes. Allow to cool briefly, add 5 tablespoons honey and $1/2$ cup (125 ml) vinegar, and cook for a further 10 minutes.

SAUCES
for leg of lamb

If you choose a recipe with little liquid, it is good to add a sauce. Mint and rosemary are popular with lamb, so here are two suggestions that incorporate these flavors.

... with ginger, yogurt, and golden raisins

Make cuts in the leg of lamb. Mix 2 tablespoons grated ginger with salt, 1 teaspoon coriander, 1 teaspoon cumin, $1/_2$ teaspoon curry powder, $1/_2$ teaspoon cayenne, 3 cloves, 1 teaspoon cardamom, 2 tablespoons lemon juice, and $5^1/_2$ oz (150 g) yogurt. Place the leg of lamb on aluminum foil, pour over the sauce, add $1^3/_4$ oz (50 g) each golden raisins and toasted slivered almonds, close the foil, and marinate for 4 hours. Cook for 2 hours in the oven, wrapped in foil, at 325 °F/160 °C.

Mint sauce

Steep finely chopped mint with sugar and boiling water in a tall container. Add vinegar and a little salt. Goes well with leg of lamb with ginger and golden raisins.

... with lime, eggs, and herbs

Bone and brown the meat, then braise for 2 hours in 6 cups (1.5 liters) bouillon with the juice and peel of 1 lime, 1 celery stalk, 1 carrot, 1 onion, 1 clove garlic, 2 bay leaves, 3 sprigs thyme, and 1 tablespoon pepper. Remove the meat. Purée 2 cloves garlic, $1/_2$ bunch thyme, $1/_2$ bunch basil, $1/_2$ bunch parsley, 5 tablespoons olive oil, and 3 tablespoons of the lime juice stock. Stir in 2 chopped hard-boiled eggs and season with salt and pepper.

Rosemary and shallot sauce

Sweat diced shallots in butter with 1 sprig rosemary. Pour on red wine and boil down almost completely. Pour on lamb stock and reduce again. Bind with flakes of ice-cold butter. Goes well with the leg of lamb with kidney beans and sweet corn, and bell pepper, honey, and saffron variations.

POULTRY

Chicken, duck, turkey, and goose—poultry is popular, very healthy, and tastes delicious.

Whether roasted, crisply fried, braised until tender, whole with stuffing, or jointed, poultry has a lot to offer.

Here, you'll find a wide and varied selection of recipes ranging from crispy chicken wings and legs through tender turkey breast.

There are also many options for varying the recipes, sauces to go with them, and fantastic side dishes.

MARINADE INFO

Marinating involves placing raw meat or fish in a flavored, often sour liquid, known as a marinade. This method results in flavors and acid deeply penetrating the food. This makes it tastier and more aromatic, while at the same time the acid effect makes the meat more tender. After marinating, meat is usually braised, fried, roasted, or broiled, while fish is sometimes used without any further preparation (for example, gravlax). Marinades are usually based on acid liquids

such as vinegar, wine, sour cream, buttermilk, or lemon juice, with added herbs and spices, vegetable oils, onions, garlic, sweet ingredients such as honey or sugar, and much more—all according to taste.

To **marinate**, pieces of meat or fish should be completely covered with liquid and the container closed to be as airtight as possible; marinating takes

hours, or even days. A short marinating time is popular for barbecue dishes, because the soaked-in flavors are protected from the heat, while surface seasoning quickly burns off.

Serves 4

8	chicken legs (4¹/₂ oz/125 g each)
1	crushed garlic clove
2 tbsp	oil
2 tbsp	soy sauce
1 tsp	chile powder
	Pepper

Step by step

Wash the chicken legs and pat dry with paper towels.

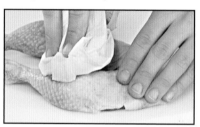

Mix the garlic with the oil, soy sauce, chile powder, and pepper.

Marinate the chicken legs for at least 1 hour.

Remove the chicken legs from the marinade and put on a wire rack in the broiler. Fill a drip pan with water and place underneath the rack.

Broil the chicken on both sides for at least 10 minutes each side, brushing frequently with the marinade.

Put the chicken on a plate and serve with rice.

CHICKEN LEGS
with soy sauce, garlic, and chile marinade

CHICKEN LEGS
several variations

When broiling or grilling, brush the meat with the marinade from time to time to prevent it from drying out and allow the delicious aromas and flavors to penetrate the meat as much as possible. Here is a choice of six different kinds of flavoring.

... with maple syrup, chilli, and balsamic vinegar marinade

For the marinade, sweat 1 finely diced onion until transparent, add 7 tablespoons (100 ml) maple syrup, 3 tablespoons chilli sauce, 2 tablespoons each white balsamic vinegar and cider vinegar, and 1 teaspoon Worcestershire sauce. Marinate the chicken legs for at least 3 hours in the icebox.

... with honey and mustard marinade

For the marinade, mix $^3/_4$ cup (175 ml) honey with 6 tablespoons whole grain mustard, 2 tablespoons white wine vinegar, and 3 tablespoons oil. Pour the marinade over the chicken legs. Cover and marinate the chicken for at least 3 hours in the icebox.

... with ketchup and cumin marinade

For the marinade, mix 1 teaspoon dry mustard, 1 tablespoon hot paprika, 1 tablespoon ground cumin, 4 tablespoons tomato ketchup, 1 tablespoon lemon juice, and salt. Gradually add 5 tablespoons melted butter. Brush the chicken legs with the marinade and marinate for at least 3 hours in the icebox.

... with mint, lime, and coconut marinade

For the marinade, mix 3 tablespoons finely chopped mint, 4 tablespoons honey, 4 tablespoons lime juice, and 4 tablespoons coconut milk with salt and pepper in a bowl. Turn the chicken legs in the marinade and marinate for at least 3 hours in the icebox.

... with lemon, sesame, and ginger marinade

For the marinade, mix together 4 tablespoons soy sauce, 6 tablespoons lemon juice, 4 tablespoons honey, 4 tablespoons sesame oil, 4 crushed cloves garlic, 2 tablespoons grated ginger, 1 teaspoon chile flakes, 3 tablespoons oil, salt and pepper. Cover and marinate the chicken legs for at least 3 hours in the icebox.

... with chile, onions, and rosemary

For the marinade, mix 3 tablespoons oil with chile powder, chopped rosemary and thyme, salt, pepper, and ground paprika. Pour over the chicken legs and marinate for 3 hours. Fry the chicken legs and and scatter with fried onion rings and chopped chiles.

SIDE DISHES
for chicken legs

Don't want to serve bread, but a "proper" side dish instead? These three suggestions give you a choice.

Parsley rice

Add double the amount of salt water for each cup of rice. Bring to a boil and simmer over low heat for about 15 minutes, until all the water has been absorbed. Stir in a few flakes of butter and plenty of chopped parsley.

Mango and cucumber tartare

Mix together finely diced mango, finely diced cucumber, and thinly sliced scallions. Mix in finely chopped cilantro, salt, and pepper, cover, and allow to stand for 30 minutes.

Bulgur

Stir $1^1/_4$ cups (250 g) bulgur into $1^1/_2$ cups (375 ml) boiling, salt water and simmer over low heat for 20 minutes. Sweat 3 tablespoons (25 g) chopped filberts and 1 finely chopped red chile in 1 tablespoon butter, and mix with the bulgur and 3 tablespoons chopped parsley. Season to taste with salt and pepper.

CHICKEN—COQ AU VIN
with red wine and scallions

INFO

For the classic **coq au vin,** you need the following: "coq" means "rooster," so you need a rooster, preferably one that's a year old and about 7 lb (3.2 kg) in weight. As these are not easy to obtain, some people use capon. This is an expensive alternate, however, so roaster chicken is often substituted. The classic recipe involves spirits as well as wine. Under no circumstances should you use an inferior wine. The same wine should be used in cooking as is served with the meal.

Serves 4

3¹/₂ tbsp (50 g)	*butter*
3¹/₂ oz (100 g)	*bacon, finely diced*
2	*onions, finely diced*
1	*chicken (2¹/₂ lb/1.2 kg), jointed into 4 pieces*
1 tbsp	*flour*
8	*scallions, sliced into rings*
2 cups (500 ml)	*dry red wine*
4 tbsp	*brandy*
1	*bay leaf*
¹/₂ tsp	*thyme*
1 pinch	*nutmeg*
	Salt
	Pepper
5¹/₂ oz (150 g)	*mushrooms*

Step by step

Melt 1 oz (25 g) of butter in a casserole. Brown the bacon and onions in the butter, remove, and put aside.

Brown the chicken joints in the casserole and dust with flour. Add the scallions and cook for a few minutes.

Pour on the wine and the brandy. Add the herbs, spices, and seasoning and braise for 30 minutes over low heat.

Clean and slice the mushrooms and sauté gently in the remaining butter for 10 minutes.

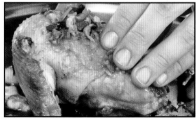

Remove the chicken portions from the pan, sieve the sauce into another pan, and heat with the mushrooms, onions, and bacon.

Side dish

Coq au vin is traditionally served with **baguette**. The bread of this long, stick-like French loaf, which is deliciously crusty when fresh, is used for dipping. This means that not a drop of the delicious sauce is lost. If you don't have a fresh baguette available at home, you can bake one from the day before. Slightly stale bread is actually even better suited to mopping up the sauce. You can, of course, also use ordinary white bread.

Side dish

With the broiled chicken legs, serve a mixture of **basmati rice and wild rice**. First, sweat $1^1/_4$ cups (250 g) mixed basmati and wild rice in 3 tablespoons butter until transparent, pour on double the quantity of liquid (chicken bouillon is best), season with salt, and simmer over low heat for 20–25 minutes. Fluff with a fork to let the steam escape and stir in 2 tablespoons flaked butter.

SIDE DISHES
for chicken

Rice and potatoes in various forms go well with chicken. Here are three suggestions:

Mashed potatoes with olive oil

Boil 1³/₄ lb (800 g) potatoes, peel, and put through a ricer while still hot. Mix with 2–3 tablespoons warm olive oil and butter, and season to taste with salt and nutmeg.

Couscous

Bring 9 oz (250 g) couscous to a boil with about double the quantity of liquid and a little salt. Simmer for a few minutes until the liquid is absorbed—and it's done!

Parsley potatoes

Peel 1³/₄ lb (800 g) potatoes and halve or quarter them. Cook in boiling, salt water for about 20 minutes until done. After cooking, leave them to stand, uncovered, in the water for a short time, to allow the steam to dissipate. Sprinkle with chopped parsley.

CHICKEN
several

For a long time, poultry—chicken in particular—was a relatively economical source of meat, as these types of fowl require comparatively little care. Even today, poultry is favorably priced. Below, we have four variations on roast or braised chicken, ranging from lemony and fresh through mild to exotic and

... with lemon, potatoes, and onions

Put the chicken portions in a casserole. Mix a marinade with the juice of 5 lemons, salt, pepper, and ¹/₂ cup (125 ml) olive oil. Arrange a generous 1 lb (500 g) small, peeled potatoes and the same amount of quartered onions on the chicken. Pour over the marinade, cover, and cook in the oven for 1 hour at 400 °F/200 °C.

... with casserole vegetables and cider

Brown the chicken portions in 6 tablespoons olive oil over high heat. Add 1 halved onion and brown lightly. Also brown 1 pack frozen casserole vegetables (or a chopped carrot, stalk of celery, and leek). Pour on generous 1¹/₂ cups (375 ml) hard cider and bring to a boil. Season to taste with bouillon, pepper, and Tabasco® Sauce. Cover, then simmer over low heat. Braise for 1 hour, turning the portions every 20 minutes.

SALADS
for chicken

variations

fiery Mexican. You can, of course, use the recipes with other kinds of poultry, but be aware of the differences in cooking times.

Simple salads and chicken go well together. And you won't need more than a fresh baguette to serve alongside them.

Quick tomato salad

Mix 8 sliced tomatoes, 2 finely chopped scallions, 2 tablespoons each white wine vinegar and oil, salt, and pepper, and allow to marinate for at least 15 minutes. Before serving, stir the salad once again.

... with banana, peas, and coconut milk

Brown the chicken portions for 15 minutes in 4 tablespoons oil in a casserole. Sprinkle with curry powder and remove. Cook 7 oz (200 g) diced carrots, 3 finely diced onions, and 2 chopped chiles in the casserole. Add 1 mashed banana, 5^1/$_2$ oz (150 g) frozen peas, generous ^{3}/$_4$ cup (200 ml) coconut milk, 1 cup (250 ml) pineapple juice, and the chicken portions. Cover and cook for 45 minutes.

Iceberg salad

Shred some iceberg lettuce. Make vinaigrette by mixing oil, vinegar, sugar, salt, and pepper, and fold it into the salad.

... with chocolate, chiles, and bell pepper

Season the chicken portions with salt and pepper and brown them in 4 tablespoons oil. Remove from the casserole, add 1 diced onion, and sweat until transparent. Add 1 tablespoon red wine. Add 1 each green bell pepper and chile, diced, plus 1^3/$_4$ lb (800 g) canned tomatoes, and bring to a boil. Stir in 1 oz (30 g) grated dark chocolate, season with salt and pepper, return the chicken to the casserole, and braise for 30 minutes.

Lollo bionda

Mix olive oil with balsamic vinegar, medium-hot mustard, salt, pepper, lemon juice, and chile powder, season to taste with chopped thyme, marjoram, and basil, and pour over the salad. Sprinkle with crunchy croutons.

STUFFED CHICKEN
with bread roll and egg

Serves 4

1	roaster chicken (about 2¹/₂ lb/1.2 kg)
	Salt
	Pepper
1	stale bread roll, diced
1	egg
	Nutmeg
3 tbsp	lukewarm milk
2 tbsp	onions, finely chopped
1 tbsp	parsley, chopped
¹/₃ cup (80 g)	butter
¹/₂	onion, coarsely chopped
1	carrot, coarsely chopped
1 tsp	sweet paprika
1 cup (250 ml)	chicken bouillon

Step by step

Wash the chicken, pat dry, and rub with salt and pepper inside and outside. Crumble the bread roll in a bowl.

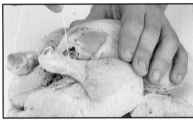

Truss the chicken with kitchen string (see Info column on the right).

Mix the egg and nutmeg with the milk, season, and pour over the roll. Sweat the finely chopped onion with the parsley in 2 tablespoons of butter.

Put the chicken in a roasting pan and pour over 6 tablespoons of melted butter. Add the vegetables, and cook for 30 minutes at 400 °F/200 °C.

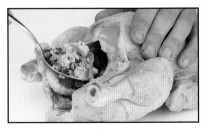

After resting the stuffing for 30 minutes, fill the chicken.

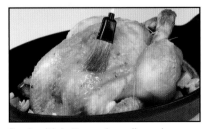

Brush with butter and paprika and remove from the pan. Deglaze with bouillon, reduce briefly, and sieve.

POULTRY INFO

If you are frying whole **poultry**, you should if possible truss them first, that is to say, tie them so that the meat will not dry out and the bird will stay in shape. Don't let yourself be put off, it really isn't very difficult! This is how you do it:

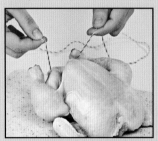

Put the chicken on its back, pass kitchen string under the parson's nose,

cross it above and wrap it once around the drumsticks, then cross it again.

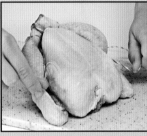

Pull the string tight, pass it behind the legs, and turn over.

In the front, put the twine around both wings, loop it behind, and pull it tight. Tie a knot—and you're done!

POULTRY

SAUCES
for chicken

Now all you need is a delicious sauce, and you'll have a very special meal that isn't served every day. Here are two suggestions for sauce options:

White wine, ginger, and cinnamon sauce

Fry diced onion until transparent, then add crushed garlic and tomato paste. Add white wine, lemon peel, grated ginger, cinnamon, sugar, and salt, simmer for 5 minutes, and thicken. Excellent with the bread roll and egg, rice and mint, and chestnut and almond stuffing variations.

Bacon, honey, and balsamic vinegar sauce

Fry the bacon until crisp. Add honey and balsamic vinegar. Bring to a boil and remove from the heat immediately. Suitable for all stuffings.

... with ground meat, bacon and cream

For the stuffing, mix $3^1/_2$ oz (100 g) ground meat with $3/_4$ oz (20 g) diced bacon. Sweat $1/_2$ onion and $1/_2$ bunch finely chopped parsley in 2 tablespoons butter, mix with $1/_2$ soaked bread roll, salt, pepper, nutmeg, rosemary, 2 tablespoons light cream, 1 egg, $1/_2$ clove crushed garlic, and the meat.

... with spinach, Parmesan, and tomato

For the filling, defrost 9 oz (250 g) chopped frozen spinach. Sweat in 2 tablespoons butter, season with salt, pepper, and nutmeg, and allow to cool. Then mix with 1 egg, 1 tablespoon grated Parmesan, and 1 finely diced tomato, plus 1 tablespoon dried breadcrumbs.

STUFFED CHICKEN
several variations

In principle, you can stuff a chicken with almost any ingredients, as long as they harmonize with one another and with the meat. The fillings listed here will, of course, go with other types of poultry; all you have to do is adjust the quantity.

... with chestnuts and almonds

For the filling, purée $2^1/_2$ oz (75 g) peeled and cooked chestnuts and mix with $^3/_4$ oz (20 g) diced bacon, 1 egg, 1 tablespoon slivered almonds, 1 tablespoon brandy, $^1/_2$ chopped onion, 1 tablespoon chopped parsley, 1 crushed clove garlic, salt, pepper, thyme, rosemary, and 1 oz (25 g) dried breadcrumbs.

... with apples, mugwort, and brandy

For the filling, peel, core, and quarter 14 oz (400 g) tart apples. Mix with $^1/_2$ chopped onion, 1 teaspoon mugwort, and 1 tablespoon brandy.

... with rice, currants, and mint

For the filling, soak $^1/_3$ cup (75 g) long-grain rice with 1 oz (30 g) currants in water for 30 minutes. Sweat 1 finely diced onion in 2 tablespoons butter and add 1 oz (30 g) pine nuts. Stir in the rice and sweat until transparent. Add $^1/_2$ cup (125 ml) water, $^1/_2$ teaspoon cinnamon, 1 pinch allspice, and 1 teaspoon salt. Cover and simmer for 15 minutes, then stir in $^1/_2$ bunch chopped parsley and the same amount of mint.

... with red onions, sage, and liver

For the filling, chop chicken liver finely and fry for a few minutes in 1 tablespoon butter. Simmer 14 oz (400 g) red onions in water for 10 minutes. Two minutes before the end of the cooking time, add 10 sage leaves. Pour off the water, allow the onions and the sage to cool, and chop very finely. Mix well with the liver, $4^1/_2$ oz (125 g) white breadcrumbs, 4 tablespoons butter, 1 egg, salt, and pepper.

CHICKEN WINGS
deep-fried with Tabasco® Sauce and paprik

Serves 4

2¼ lb (1 kg)	chicken wings, (about 16 wings)
2 cups (500 ml)	oil for frying
3 tbsp	butter
1 tbsp	lemon juice
2 tbsp	Tabasco® Sauce
1 tsp	sweet paprika
1 pinch	chile powder

Step by step

Wash the chicken wings and cut through the middles.

Remove the chicken wings with a slotted spoon and drain well on paper towels. Arrange in a bowl.

Heat the oil in a heavy skillet for frying.

Melt the butter and stir in the lemon juice, Tabasco® Sauce, paprika, and chile powder.

Fry the chicken wings in batches for 8–10 minutes until golden brown, turning once.

Drizzle the sauce over the chicken wings in the bowl.

TABASCO INFO

Tabasco is a very hot chilli sauce based on a special type of chile cultivated by the McIlhenny Company, who also produce the sauce. The exact production process and recipe for Tabasco® Sauce is a strictly kept company secret.

All that is known is that the sauce consists only of vinegar, crushed, ripe chiles, and salt, without artificial preservatives or coloring. The special flavor comes from the fermentation process that the chilli sauce undergoes for up to three years in oak barrels. All bottles of Tabasco® Sauce sold worldwide are filled in Avery Island, and the recipe used is always the same. In 1920, a law still valid today decreed that the only company allowed to produce Tabasco® Sauce was the McIlhenny Company, and that they might even name sauces "Tabasco" that did not contain any chiles of the Tabasco variety. Patent protection of the method of production has now expired, so other manufacturers may sell sauces produced by similar methods. These are usually termed "Louisiana Style" and may indicate that they are made from Tabasco chiles.

DIPS
for chicken wings

First soaked in a delicious marinade, then broiled or grilled, and finally served with a dip: that's what makes crispy chicken wings irresistible.

BBQ dip

Sweat diced onion in oil until transparent, add 1 teaspoon brown sugar, and caramelize. Pour over 2 tablespoons cider vinegar and 9 oz (250 g) canned tomatoes, and reduce. Season with salt, pepper, and Tabasco® Sauce. Excellent with the chicken wings with Tabasco® Sauce and paprika, and Fanta®, Coca-Cola®, and peach marinade variations.

Cream cheese and Tabasco® Sauce dip

Mix 7 oz (200 g) cream cheese with 7 tablespoons (100 ml) yogurt. Stir in 2 tablespoons ketchup, sweet paprika, Worcestershire sauce, and Tabasco® Sauce. Goes well with the chicken wings with Tabasco® Sauce and paprika, and with chile and star anise recipe variations.

Basil dip

Mix together 1 cup (250 ml) sour cream and 2 tablespoons salad cream, and season with salt and pepper. Stir in chopped basil. Excellent with chicken wings with Tabasco® Sauce and paprika, and with garlic and lime marinade.

CHICKEN WINGS
several

We don't know when chicken wings first appeared as a dish. It was definitely in the United States. The question of whether it was during the years before the Civil War, however, or not until later—in a bar in Buffalo, as a way of using up leftovers—remains open. The fact is that deliciously marinated, grilled or

... with honey, ketchup, and ginger marinade

Mix 5 tablespoons each honey and tomato ketchup with 3 tablespoons soy sauce. Season with $^{1}/_{2}$ teaspoon each ginger and thyme. Brush the chicken wings with some of the marinade, cover, and leave to marinate for 1 hour in the icebox. Place on a broiler rack, stand in a drip pan of water, and cook in the oven at 400 °F/200 °C for 20–30 minutes. Halfway through the cooking time, brush the wings with more marinade.

... with chiles, soy sauce, and star anise

Briefly fry 1 slice ginger in 2 tablespoons oil. Add the chicken wings, brown, and season with salt and pepper. Briefly fry 2 roughly chopped, dried chiles with the chicken wings. Add 1 tablespoon sugar, but do not let it brown. Pour on 1 tablespoon soy sauce and half-cover the chicken wings with water. Add 1 stick cinnamon and 1 piece star anise, and simmer for 30 minutes.

DIPS
for chicken wings

variations

deep-fried chicken wings have long been seen, not as "leftovers," but as a popular finger food. They can be bought fresh or frozen, are easy to make, and delightfully crispy. Here, we have a few recipes for various ways of serving chicken wings, and also for some tasty dips.

Do you prefer them spicy and creamy, or mild and creamy with plenty of garlic? The decision is yours!

Yogurt and quark dip with onions and garlic
Combine 7 tablespoons (100 ml) yogurt with the same amount of quark and sour cream. Season with salt and pepper. Mix with 2 very finely chopped raw onions and 1 crushed garlic clove. Goes well with the chicken wings with Tabasco® Sauce and paprika, garlic and lime marinade, and chile and star anise recipe variations.

... with garlic, lime, and orange marinade
Prepare a marinade with 2 crushed cloves garlic, the juice of 2 limes and 1 orange, 2 tablespoons chile powder, 2 soaked, dried, and puréed chiles, 2 tablespoons oil, 1 teaspoon sugar, $^1/_4$ teaspoon allspice, cumin, and oregano. Marinate for at least 3 hours, then grill or broil.

Herby cream cheese and cream dip
Beat together 9 oz (250 g) herb cream cheese (e.g. Boursin®) with 7 tablespoons (100 ml) light cream. Season to taste with pepper. Suitable for all the recipe variations.

... with Fanta®, Coca-Cola®, and peach marinade
Mix 1 finely chopped chile and 2 crushed garlic cloves with $^2/_3$ cup (150 ml) Fanta®, 5 $^1/_2$ oz (150 g) peach jelly, 5 tablespoons mustard, 1 tablespoon soy sauce, and 4 tablespoons Coca-Cola®. Marinate the chicken wings for 1 hour in the mixture, remove, and season with salt and pepper. Broil or grill for 15 minutes, turning once. Heat the marinade and add 2 tablespoons sour cream.

Garlic dip
Cook garlic cloves for 15 minutes in salt water, drain, and push through a sieve. Stir until creamy with chicken bouillon. Season to taste with salt and pepper. Goes well with the chicken wings with Tabasco® Sauce and paprika, garlic and lime marinade, and Fanta®, Coca-Cola®, and peach marinade variations.

TURKEY ESCALOPES AU GRATIN
with cherry tomatoes and mozzarella

INFO

Mozzarella, a white cheese of Italian origin, is widespread today and made in many places all over the world. Mozzarella is most often made from cow's milk, but do try buffalo mozzarella, which is more aromatic. The cheese gets its consistency from a special method of cheese-making, where the curd, after a period of resting, has hot water poured over it and is made into a shapeable dough by kneading, pulling, and stirring. Afterward, the cheese "dough" is placed in brine.

Serves 4

4	turkey escalopes (about 5$^1/_2$ oz/150 g each)
	Salt
	Pepper
3 tbsp	oil
5$^1/_2$ oz (150 g)	cherry tomatoes, halved
4$^1/_2$ oz (125 g)	mozzarella, cut into 8 slices
$^1/_2$ bunch	basil

Step by step

Wash the turkey escalopes and pat dry with paper towels. Rub with salt and pepper.

Brown the escalopes for about 5 minutes each side in 3 tablespoons of oil.

In the pan, cover the escalopes with halved cherry tomatoes, season, put 2 slices of mozzarella on each escalope, and sprinkle with pepper.

Put the pan in the broiler and broil for 5–10 minutes, or cover with a lid over low heat and allow the cheese to melt.

Garnish the turkey escalopes with basil leaves, and serve.

Side dish

Garlic toast makes a great accompaniment. Mix 1$^1/_2$ tablespoons (25 g) garlic butter, 1$^1/_2$ tablespoons (25 g) softened butter, $^1/_2$ teaspoon salt, 1 small chopped onion, 1 crushed garlic clove, and a little chopped parsley. Lightly toast 6 slices of bread, spread with the garlic butter mixture, and cut in half. Then bake them in the oven for about 10 minutes.

Salad

Also excellent with turkey escalopes au gratin is a crunchy **iceberg salad**. Mix the shredded leaves of one head iceberg lettuce with 9 oz (250 g) canned mandarin oranges. For the dressing, mix 2 tablespoons (30 g) crème fraîche with the juice of 1 lemon, 4 tablespoons mandarin juice from the can, salt, and pepper. Combine well with the salad.

TURKEY ESCALOPES AU GRATIN
several variations

Cheddar, Parmesan, Emmental, or goat's cheese—combining it with a turkey escalope makes any cheese special. Don't over-bake the escalopes. Just let the cheese gently turn golden brown or simply melt—that gives it the best flavor.

... with peach, goat's cheese, and mint
Rub the turkey escalopes with Chinese five-spice powder and fry. Place on a baking sheet and cover with 14 oz (400 g) canned peach halves and 2 slices goat's cheese per escalope. Bake at 400 °F/200 °C for 15–20 minutes, until the cheese is golden brown. Sprinkle with the torn leaves of 3 mint sprigs.

... with pineapple, cranberries, and Cheddar
Put the turkey escalopes in a shallow ovenproof dish and pour over a mixture of 1 cup (250 ml) light cream, salt, and pepper. Top each escalope with 1 slice each pineapple and Cheddar cheese. Bake at 400 °F/200 °C for 15–20 minutes. Then top each escalope with 1 teaspoon cranberries.

... with spinach and Emmental
Season the turkey escalopes and put them in an ovenproof dish. Thaw 1 pack frozen leaf spinach, season with salt and nutmeg, and top the escalopes with it. Beat together 2 eggs and 4 tablespoons cream cheese until smooth, and distribute over the meat. Sprinkle with 3^1/$_2$ oz (100 g) grated Emmental and bake at 400 °F/200 °C for 15–20 minutes.

... with boiled ham, asparagus, and Gouda
Brown the turkey escalopes, remove from the pan, and top each one with 1 slice boiled ham, 2 cooked asparagus stalks cut into pieces, and 1 slice Gouda cheese. Bake at 400 °F/200 °C for 15–20 minutes.

SAUCES
for turkey escalopes

To accompany turkey escalopes that are simply fried in oil or clarified butter, whether whole, diced, or in goujons, you can use sauces with a wide range of flavors. Here are a few suggestions, ranging from mild through hot:

Mango and brandy sauce

Crush 9 oz (250 g) canned sweetened mangoes together with the juice in a pan. Add 1 tablespoon brandy and $^1/_2$ teaspoon grated ginger, reduce till thickened, and season with salt and pepper. Excellent with the turkey escalopes with peach and mint, pineapple and cranberries, and mushrooms and Parmesan recipe variations.

Yogurt and mustard sauce

Mix 1 cup (250 ml) yogurt with 1–2 tablespoons medium–hot mustard and Italian herbs, stir until smooth, then season with salt and pepper. Goes well with the turkey escalopes with mushrooms and Parmesan, spinach and Emmental, and tomatoes and cream cheese variations.

Fruity curry sauce

Sweat 2 tablespoons butter with 2 tablespoons flour, add a little water, and bring to a boil. Add half the juice of $3^1/_2$ oz (100 g) each canned pineapple and canned peaches. Season with salt and curry powder. Add the diced canned fruit. Excellent with the turkey escalopes with peach and mint, pineapple and cranberries, and mushrooms and Parmesan variations.

... with mushrooms, sherry, and Parmesan

Lightly sauté 14 oz (400 g) sliced mushrooms in butter and season with salt. Brown the escalopes over high heat, reduce the heat, and fry for 5 minutes. Deglaze the pan with 4 table-spoons sherry and add 3 tablespoons butter. Put the escalopes in a baking dish, cover with the mushrooms, pour over the pan juices, sprinkle with 4 tablespoons grated Parmesan, and bake at 400 °F/200 °C for 15–20 minutes.

... with tomatoes, and cream cheese with chives

Brown the turkey escalopes and place in a baking dish. Top with 3 sliced tomatoes. Beat together $5^1/_2$ oz (150 g) cream cheese, 1 chopped bunch chives, and 1 egg yolk. Season to taste with salt and pepper and spread evenly over the tomatoes. Bake at 400 °F/200 °C for 15–20 minutes.

SOY SAUCE INFO

Soy sauce is a mixture of roasted and ground soy beans, wheat germ, water, and salt, made into soy sauce with certain fermentation procedures covering different lengths of time.

The traditional Japanese soy sauce is light or dark, without any additives.

Ketjap Manis is a sweetish soy sauce from Indonesia.

Certain soy sauces also have molasses added, to give them a darker color.

Serves 4

5 tbsp	oil
generous 1 lb (500 g)	turkey breast, cut into strips
2	red bell peppers, cut into strips
2	yellow bell peppers, cut into strips
3½ oz (100 g)	soy bean sprouts
5	leaves Swiss chard, cut into strips
4 tbsp	soy sauce
2 tbsp	white wine vinegar
	Salt
1 tbsp	sweet paprika
6 tbsp	sweet soy sauce (Ketjap Manis)
1 tsp	brown sugar
1 tsp	corn starch
2 tbsp	sesame seeds

Step by step

Heat the oil in a wok or pan, brown the turkey breast on all sides, then remove or push to the side of the pan.

Add the soy sauce and vinegar, and bring to a boil.

Add the strips of bell pepper, brown, and also remove or push to the side.

Lightly incorporate the strips of turkey and bell pepper.

Then do the same with the soy bean sprouts and Swiss chard.

Season with salt, paprika, sweet soy sauce, and brown sugar. Thicken with the corn-starch and sprinkle with sesame seeds.

TURKEY BREAST
with soy bean sprouts and Swiss chard

POULTRY

SIDE DISHES
for turkey breast

These savory vegetable dishes with bell peppers and onions are simply delicious! And perfectly suited to mild-flavored turkey breast.

Peperonata

Sweat thin slices of onion in oil until transparent, then add quartered, mixed, colored bell peppers and sliced garlic. Drizzle with white wine vinegar and bring briefly to a boil. Season with cayenne, salt, and pepper, add quartered, peeled tomatoes and 2 tablespoons granulated sugar, and simmer for 20 minutes. Do not allow the vegetables to become too soft.

Lecsó

Sweat green bell peppers cut into strips with onions sliced into rings, in plenty of oil. Add peeled and seeded tomatoes, season with salt, pepper, sweet paprika, and sugar, and heat gently.

TURKEY BREAST
several

Turkey is very popular because of its excellent qualities: the white meat is pleasantly mild, making it suitable for a wide range of cooking and serving; its low fat content makes it easy to digest; it contains many essential vitamins and minerals; and it has an ideal protein composition. Cut into strips,

... with carrots, cream, and basil

Fry diced turkey breast in 2 tablespoons oil until golden brown, season, and remove from the pan. Sweat generous 1 lb (500 g) sliced carrots, 2 onions sliced into rings, and 2 crushed cloves garlic for 5 minutes. Bring to a boil with 2 cups (500 ml) each chicken bouillon and light cream. Add the turkey and simmer for 15 minutes. Just before the end of the cooking time, add 1 bunch chopped basil.

... with oranges, kiwi fruit, and raisins

Rub the meat with 1 crushed clove garlic, chile powder, allspice, and cinnamon. Fry until brown. Pour on water and add the juice of 1 orange mixed with 1 teaspoon honey, $^1/_2$ teaspoon allspice, 1 teaspoon ground ginger, and $^1/_2$ teaspoon curry powder. Fry 1 diced kiwi fruit with $1^3/_4$ oz (50 g) raisins, pour on the juice of 3 oranges, and season with ginger, curry powder, and garlic. Add to the sauce and reduce.

SIDE DISHES
for turkey breast

diced, in slices, or as a whole piece—these sample recipes will show you a few ways of making the most of the delicate white meat of turkey breast.

Wonderfully sweet, yet hearty: these onion dishes taste particularly good with turkey breast—either as a purée, delicately refined with butter, or as whole shallots glazed with sugar.

... with white wine, milk, and sage

In a casserole, fry the turkey breast over high heat in 2 table-spoons olive oil. Briefly fry 12 sage leaves, cut into strips, the chopped leaves of 3 rosemary sprigs, and 3 thyme sprigs. Pour on generous $^3/_4$ cup (200 ml) white wine and 4 cups (1 liter) milk. Cook in the oven for about 1 hour at 350 °F/180 °C, turning the meat during cooking. Mix the sauce with a handheld blender until creamy and thick.

Onion purée

Cook slices of white Spanish onion in meat bouillon until soft, then purée. Stir in light cream, bring to a boil, and season with salt and pepper. Then stir in cold butter and serve.

... with tomatoes, artichokes, and capers

Brown sliced turkey breast and season with salt and pepper. Top the turkey slices with 4 peeled, sliced tomatoes, 9 oz (250 g) canned artichoke hearts, cut into eighths, and 2 tablespoons capers. Mix 3 tablespoons each lemon juice and oil with 1 crushed garlic clove and spread the mixture over the meat. Sprinkle with $3^1/_2$ oz (100 g) grated Gouda and bake in the oven at 400 °F/200 °C for 25 minutes.

Glazed shallots

Caramelize peeled shallots in hot butter and sugar, and add bouillon. Cook until the shallots are soft and the liquid has evaporated.

ROAST DUCK
with orange, honey, and thyme

	Serves 4
1	*oven-ready duck (5 lb/2.25 kg)*
	Salt
	Pepper
5 sprigs	*thyme*
²/₃ cup (150 ml)	*orange juice*
1¹/₄ cups (300 ml)	*chicken bouillon*
¹/₂ tsp	*cinnamon*
1 tbsp	*honey*
2 tsp	*cornstarch*
4	*oranges, peeled and sliced*

Step by step

Wash the duck and pat dry. Rub with salt and pepper, and stuff the duck with the thyme.

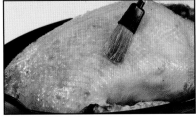

Mix the honey with 2 tablespoons of the pan juices and baste the duck with it several times (but not during the last 15 minutes).

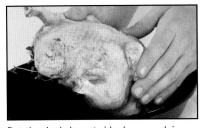

Put the duck, breast side downward, in a roasting pan, and roast in the oven at 350 °F/180 °C for about 45 minutes.

Remove the duck and deglaze the roasting pan with water. Add the cornstarch, stirred into a little water.

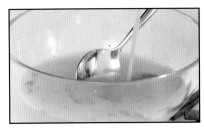

Turn the duck over. Mix together the orange juice, chicken bouillon, and cinnamon, pour over the duck, and roast for another 45 minutes.

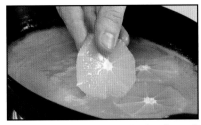

Bring the sauce to a boil, add the slices of orange, and serve with the duck.

DUCK INFO

For cooking purposes, we differentiate between wild and domesticated ducks. The Barbary duck is in a separate category, coming somewhere between **ducks** and geese.

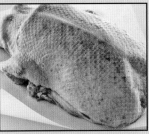

In general, **domesticated ducks** have rather more fat than their wild relations. Females are juicier and more aromatic than drakes—which, however, compensate with more depth of flavor.

Wild duck is most commonly mallard. Its meat is dark red, juicy, aromatic, and full of flavor. Often, only the duck breast is used, although the whole duck can also be stuffed.

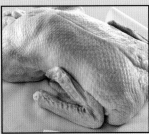

Barbary and **Muscovy ducks** have less fat and particularly delicately flavored breast meat. Ducks should not be too old be-cause, even after the first year, the meat begins to taste oily. You can recognize young, fresh, wild duck by its pale grey feet.

SIDE DISHES
for duck

Sautéed Brussels sprouts, creamy savoy cabbage, or sauerkraut with bacon—all kinds of cabbage go well with the intense flavor of duck meat.

Brussels sprouts

Make a cross-shaped cut in the stalks of generous 1 lb (500 g) Brussels sprouts, sweat in oil, and season with salt and pepper. Pour on 2 cups of bouillon, cover, and simmer for 10 minutes until soft. Season to taste with nutmeg and stir in flakes of butter.

Savoy cabbage in cream sauce

Cut 1 savoy cabbage into strips and blanch. Sweat diced onions and crushed garlic clove, and dust with flour. Pour on bouillon, white wine, and light cream, and season with salt, pepper, and nutmeg. Add the cabbage and simmer for a few minutes. Season to taste with lemon juice.

Silesian sauerkraut

Bring generous 1 lb (500 g) sauerkraut to a boil in water, cover, and simmer for 20 minutes. Strain, pressing the liquid out well. Fry 3$\frac{1}{2}$ oz (100 g) diced onion and bacon until the onions are transparent; add the sauerkraut and simmer for a further 20 minutes.

... with apples, rosemary, and currants

Rub the duck with salt and pepper. Peel and core 2 apples, and cut them into wedges. Stuff the duck with the apples, 1 sprig rosemary, and 1 oz (30 g) currants, and secure with toothpicks. Roast in the oven for 15 minutes, add 2 cups (500 ml) bouillon, and turn the duck over. Continue roasting, basting several times.

... with quince, bacon, and white wine

Rub the duck with salt, pepper, and marjoram, and cover the breast and legs with 3$\frac{1}{2}$ oz (100 g) smoked bacon rashers. Stuff the duck with 2 peeled quince cut into eighths and secure with toothpicks. Pour over 3 tablespoons hot goose fat and roast. Peel 4 quince, cut into eighths, simmer with 7 tablespoons (100 ml) white wine, cloves, cinnamon, and 2 tablespoons sugar until cooked, and distribute around the duck.

ROAST DUCK
several variations

Each of these dishes deserves to be served at a special occasion. Decide for yourself which variation you like best. You can, of course, prepare other poultry, such as goose, in the same ways.

... with red wine and shallots

Rub the duck with salt and pepper and brown in a roasting pan. Remove, brown 9 oz (250 g) shallots in the pan, then remove them. In the pan, fry 10 juniper berries with 2 tablespoons tomato paste, then pour on 1 cup (250 ml) red wine and 2 cups (500 ml) chicken bouillon. Add the shallots and the duck, and roast. Skim the fat off the sauce, adjust the seasoning, and thicken if required.

... with avocado, banana, and red onions

Rub the duck with salt, pepper, and paprika. Mix 3 puréed bananas, 2 puréed soft avocado, and 3 finely chopped red onions with salt and pepper. Stuff the duck with the mixture and secure with toothpicks. Brown in a roasting pan and finish roasting in the oven. Deglaze the pan with 2 tablespoons tomato paste, 1 tablespoon lemon juice, and 1 tablespoon brandy; reduce till thickened, and season with salt and pepper.

... with ginger and leeks

Rub the duck with salt and pepper. Stuff with 3 teaspoons grated ginger and the very finely diced white part of 1 leek. Mix together 3 tablespoons honey and 1 tablespoon vinegar, and brush the duck with this. Roast the duck in a roasting pan, basting from time to time with the honey mixture. Garnish with 2 very finely sliced leeks sautéed in 2 tablespoons butter.

... with ground pork, dried fruit, and onions

Dice 9 oz (250 g) dried fruit soaked in apple juice, and mix with 14 oz (400 g) ground pork, 1 each diced onion and apple, and 2 tablespoons mustard. Stuff the duck with the mixture. Put 1 apple and 1 red onion, each cut into wedges, in the roasting pan with the duck. Pour in 3^1/$_4$ cups (750 ml) duck stock and roast, covered. When cooked, brush the duck with 5 tablespoons each butter and honey, and broil. Season the sauce to taste with light cream and orange juice.

STUFFED GOOSE
with chestnuts and apples

INFO

Goose fat is the cold, solidified dripping from a roasted goose. It is excellent for roasting and frying meat and vegetables. As it contains unsaturated fats, it is healthier than many other fats, on a level comparable with olive oil. It also has a very aromatic, intense flavor. Add sautéed pieces of apple and onion and make a fine spread for sandwiches and toast.

Serves 4

2	*carrots*
2	*apples*
3 tbsp	*oil*
11 oz (300 g)	*chestnuts, peeled and cooked*
$^1/_2$ bunch	*thyme, chopped*
$^1/_2$ bunch	*marjoram, chopped*
1	*oven-ready goose (about 9 lb/4 kg)*
	Salt
	Pepper
	Toothpicks

Step by step

For the filling, peel the carrots, peel and core the apples, and dice them all.

Heat 2 tablespoons of oil and sweat the carrots and apples in it. Add the halved chestnuts and herbs.

Season the goose, inside and out, with salt and pepper. Stuff the body cavity with the filling.

Close the body cavity of the goose with toothpicks.

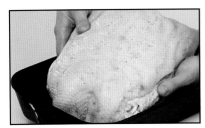

Put the goose in a roasting pan. Brush with 1 tablespoon of oil and roast in the oven at 350 °F/180 °C for about 2^1/$_2$ hours.

Side dish

Duchess potatoes are a delicious side dish for stuffed goose. To make, cook 1^3/$_4$ lb (800 g) mealy potatoes, of roughly equal size, in their skins. Peel, then put through a ricer. Stir 7 tablespoons (100 g) butter, 4 egg yolks, salt, pepper, and nutmeg into the mashed potatoes.

Spoon the potatoes into a pastry bag and pipe little piles onto a greased baking sheet. Brush with beaten egg yolk and bake at 425 °F/220 °C for 10 minutes, until the duchess potatoes take on a golden-brown color.

Side dish

Another excellent side dish is home-cooked **red cabbage**. Wash 1^3/$_4$ lb (750 g) red cabbage, cut out the hard part of the stalk, and slice the cabbage very finely. Peel, core, and finely dice 2 apples. Peel and chop 1 onion. Sweat in 2 tablespoons hot goose fat until transparent. Add the red cabbage and apple, and sweat briefly. Add ^{1}/$_2$ bay leaf, 2 juniper berries, 1 clove, 2 peppercorns, and 2 table-spoons sugar, stir in 7 tablespoons (100 ml) red wine and 1 tablespoon red wine vinegar, and simmer for 45 minutes.

SAUCES
for goose

With a crispy goose with dumplings, you need a sauce. Along with the classic roast meat gravy, try one of the following three suggestions:

Rosemary sauce

Skim the fat from the goose juices and deglaze the roasting pan with water and red wine. Mix with diced, sautéed onions and chopped rosemary. Season to taste with honey. Reduce a little.

Mustard sauce

Skim the fat from the goose juices and deglaze the roasting pan with water or white wine. Season to taste (it should be spicy) with mustard, and reduce with light cream.

Dried fruit sauce

Skim the fat from the goose juices and deglaze the roasting pan with apple wine. Add dried fruit (apples, apricots, prunes) chopped small and simmer in the stock and wine for 10 minutes.

STUFFED GOOSE
several

Goose meat has the highest fat content of all poultry meats. But when roasted in the oven, much of the fat drips into the roasting tray and can be re-used as goose fat. So you don't need to ban roast goose from the menu because of the fat content. With its crispy skin and delicious fillings such as

... with apple and celery filling

Fry $4^1/_2$ oz (125 g) diced bacon in a skillet until crisp. Remove. Sweat 1 diced celery stalk, 2 chopped onions, and 3 tablespoons parsley in the bacon fat. Remove. Sweat 5 peeled and diced apples in the bacon fat with 3 tablespoons sugar until soft. Mix together the vegetables, bacon, and $3^1/_2$ oz (100 g) bread-crumbs, and season with salt.

... with sauerkraut and bacon filling

Mix $4^1/_2$ oz (125 g) diced bacon with generous 1 lb (500 g) canned sauerkraut, 2 peeled and diced apples, and 8 juniper berries. Stuff the goose with the mixture. Crush 4 juniper berries, marinate in 4 tablespoons gin, and brush the goose with the gin and juniper berries before roasting.

variations

apple and celery, potatoes and kale, sauerkraut and bacon, or breadcrumb dumplings, roast, stuffed goose is worth those few extra calories.

SIDE DISHES
for goose

Here, we'll show you how to make potato dumplings with herbs or with bacon, and how to make liver dumplings.

Potato and herb dumplings

Cook 2¼ lb (1 kg) potatoes in their skins, drain, peel, and put through a ricer. Mix with generous 1 cup (150 g) flour, 2 eggs, and 5 tablespoons mixed, chopped herbs. Shape into dumplings and simmer in boiling, salt water for about 20 minutes.

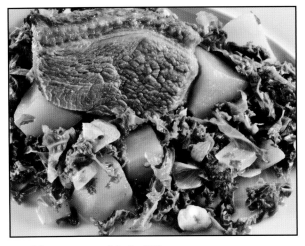

... with potato and kale filling

Fry 3½ oz (100 g) diced bacon in 2 tablespoons oil, then remove from the pan. Simmer ¾ lb (350 g) peeled and diced potatoes, 2 chopped onions, and 11 oz (300 g) shredded kale in the bacon fat for 20 minutes, until soft. Mix in the bacon and season to taste with salt and pepper.

Liver dumplings

Cook 2¼ lb (1 kg) potatoes in their skins, drain, peel, and put through a ricer. Mix with 3 cups (150 g) breadcrumbs and 3½ oz (100 g) puréed ox liver. Shape into dumplings.

... with breadcrumb dumpling filling

Dice generous 1 lb (500 g) stale white bread, fry until golden brown in 8½ tablespoons (125 g) butter, then remove from the pan. Mix the diced bread with 1¼ cups (300 ml) warmed light cream, 5 eggs, 1 bunch chopped flat-leaf parsley, and 3½ oz (100 g) ground nuts. Season to taste with salt and pepper, and stuff the goose with this mixture.

Bacon dumplings

Cook 2¼ lb (1 kg) potatoes in their skins, drain, peel, and put through a ricer. Mix with generous 1 cup (150 g) flour, 2 eggs, and 4½ oz (125 g) finely chopped fried bacon. Prepare the dumplings as described above.

Index of recipes

Index of recipes